THE

BOXING
MANUAL

The author using the pads while coaching a novice boxer

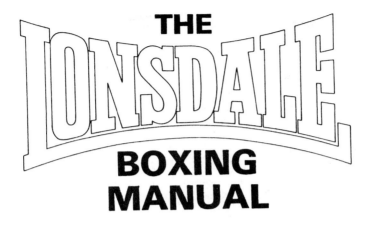

THE
BOXING
MANUAL

David James

Foreword by Harry Carpenter

 Robson Books

This edition first published in 2001 by Robson Books, 10 Blenheim Court, Brewery Road, London N7 9NY. First published in Great Britain in 1987.

British Library Cataloguing in Publication Data

A catalogue record for this book is available from the British Library

ISBN 0 86051 913 9

Printed in Great Britain by St Edmundsbury Press Ltd, Bury St Edmunds, Suffolk.

Contents

Acknowledgements

The author and publishers wish to thank Terry Marsh, I.B.F. World Champion and British, Commonwealth and European Light Welterweight Champion, for allowing his training routines to be photographed.

The publishers also gratefully acknowledge Derek Rowe for his skill and assistance in producing the technical photographs in this manual, Ray Newsam for his photographic help; and Bill Chevalley for his help in the hand-bandaging section. Dr Stephen Bird, exercise physiologist, Christchurch College, has kindly contributed advice, and John Lear, Director of Coaching B.A.W.L.A. has given valuable assistance with the section on weight training, while Sports Nutrition Consultant Justine Cotterill has made an authoritative contribution on the use of MAXIM in the weight reduction process.

The Fisher Amateur Boxing Club, Bermondsey, generously made their gym available.

Foreword by Harry Carpenter

A tattered 5×3 index card lifted from my amateur boxing files bears the heading: 'JAMES, David: Birkenhead ABC, light-heavy', and one of the earliest entries on it is dated 1959.

That is when I first saw David James – the author of this manual – box, at the old Liverpool Stadium, on a show organised by the local Litherland Club. His opponent was Johnny Ould of Bermondsey – then the reigning ABA light-heavyweight champion, and who later turned pro. Ould won on points, but later that season James won the Welsh ABA title, and it took Jack Bodell to edge him out of the national championships in the quarter-finals.

Following ten years as the Director of Sport and Recreation at the University of Kent in Canterbury, David James is now a coaching consultant. He has never lost his love of boxing, and his expertise in it is recognised worldwide. Hence this book – his own experiences have contributed to it, for he had more than a hundred amateur contests before retiring from competition in 1965. One or two of them were televised by the BBC, and I did the commentaries. I am still doing commentaries, but he has moved up in the world – as I always knew he would.

In 1967 he became the first national coach ever appointed by the Amateur Boxing Association, where he laid the foundation of today's coach education scheme and the national squad policy at both junior and senior levels, taking Great Britain's boxing teams to the Olympic Games in 1968 and 1972. Chris Finnegan won the middleweight gold medal at the 1968 Mexico Games, the last British boxer to achieve this honour, and I cannot think of anyone better qualified to instruct a young boxer in first principles than Finnegan's former Olympic coach.

David James has written a manual founded on long study and experience and, knowing the author, I am certain it is offered in a sincere belief that boxing, undertaken purely as sport, can enhance the quality of a young life. Teaching a boy to box imposes a heavy responsibility. Worthwhile textbooks are few and far between, which makes this one all the more welcome. Coaches and trainers needing a reliable reference book will find it here. A father who places this manual in the hands of his son can do so assured that the advice contained within is correct – and safe. The methods have been tried and can be trusted.

The sport may be under attack from sections of the medical profession, but David James still holds the boxing banner aloft, firmly believing that boxing has a valid place in our society because of the proper attention to fitness it demands, and the skills it develops. I am sure he is right.

The index card is going back in the box. It may be some time before it sees the light of day again. Happily, my friendship with – and respect for – David James continue day by day.

H.C., February 1994

Making a Start

Throughout the ages, boxing has progressed and developed from brutal bare-knuckle fighting to the present-day sport at both amateur and professional level where contests of skill and strength are under strict medical control. In spite of recent hysterical attacks, to young and old alike boxing remains a fascinating art and a permanent part of the country's sporting heritage. Boxing is still very much a game of skill, the art of self defence, which like any other art must be studied diligently if success is to be achieved. Boxing skill alone will not stand the young competitor in good stead unless it is backed up by courage and a level of physical fitness demanded by no other sport.

Any young hopeful who wishes to take up the sport must realise that there is no short cut to success; there are many skilled movements to learn and he must be prepared to condition his body in a hard but satisfying progressive training routine.

But first of all, he must find out the whereabouts of his nearest amateur boxing club (a list at the back of this book gives addresses of A.B.A. Provincial Associations – the secretaries will be pleased to forward you details on enquiry).

Most boxing clubs operate on at least three evenings a week, and Sunday mornings as well. From the outset, the young boxer must be prepared to attend every session and to follow the running programme that the coach will lay down for the non-club evenings.

To the young boxer, the coach now becomes an important figure in his life. The coach will plan a programme of skill coaching and fitness training that will prepare the boxer for ultimate success in the ring. The good coach will look ahead and define all-important targets or goals for the young aspirant to set his sights on. There will, however, be no escape from the overriding need to work at the basic skills of boxing. This book outlines some of the basics that every aspiring world champion should master if he is to make progress in his chosen sport.

Boxing Skills

In all probability, the coach will point out to the young boxer that the basic philosophy of the boxing art is to hit and not be hit in return. He will then outline the target on which points are scored and show the knuckle part of the glove which does the scoring.

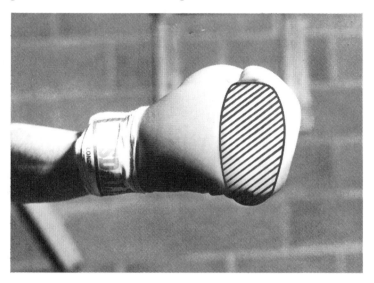

The knuckle part of the glove

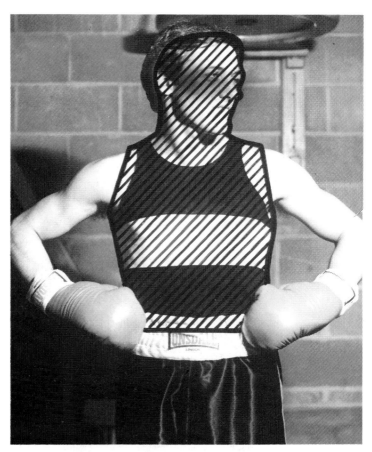

The target area for scoring punches

1. A Basic Stance
A Firm Base

Where hitting is involved in any sport, it is vital that all movements are performed from a firm base or platform formed by the feet. Throughout all punching movements, it

12

is essential that the bodyweight remains over the feet. In other words, the boxer should be able to punch singly or in combinations without disturbing his balance. Here is the best way to acquire a suitable individual base.

1. Stand with the feet shoulder width apart and take a striding pace forward with the left foot. (If you are a left-hander or 'southpaw' the opposite movements must be made.)

2. Turn the body and feet to the right in a sideways position to protect the target.

3. The bodyweight is evenly distributed between both feet – the weight is balanced on the balls of the feet,

The basic stance from the closed side

with the front foot perhaps a little flatter.

4. The rear heel is raised and this foot is offset to the right. It is the ball of this foot which is the anchor-point for most punches.

5. Both knees should be slightly bent to act as shock absorbers.

A short period of trial and error should enable the boxer to find the foot spacing that will enable him to move his upper body forward or back to the full limit without losing balance.

Upper Body

The trunk should be kept as upright as possible to enable the hips and shoulders to pivot when punching. The body-weight should be maintained over the feet, and the shoulder should afford comfortable protection for the chin without contorting into a strained position. Remember the boxer is also concerned with protecting the target area by keeping sideways to his opponent.

Hands

1. The right hand or guarding hand is carried offset from the right collar-bone. The hand is loosely clenched, ready to attack or defend.

2. The left hand is carried in the same plane, with the knuckles loosely clenched and the wrist turned slightly inward. This hand may be carried below shoulder height, according to individual preference. The chin can easily be protected by turning the left shoulder inward when the opponent throws a right hand.

3. Both elbows should be comfortably tucked in to protect the ribs.

Head

The head should be kept still with eyes fixed on the opponent. Look through the eyebrows and try and focus on the target area from the chest up.

Left: An open side view of the basic stance

2. How to Punch

Imagine that a steel rod has been driven through the head and midline of the body into the floor. All punches are produced by pivoting the body round this rod or central axis. The arms merely act as the vehicles of force produced by this central pivoting action.

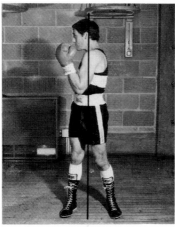

Pivoting round the central axis

3. Footwork

Having practised establishing a comfortable stance which allows him to move the upper body forward, backward and to the side without loss of balance, the boxer must now learn to move this firm base around the ring in any direction. This, of course, is where his footwork comes in. He should be able to attack or defend from a balanced position at any given time.

Foot movements should consist of short sliding steps on the balls of the feet, observing the golden rule that the feet should never cross. When moving left, the left foot leads off first, when moving right, the right foot, and when retreating, the rear foot moves off first. When moving backwards it is important that the rear foot slides back a generous distance to maintain a firm base to launch the counter-punches.

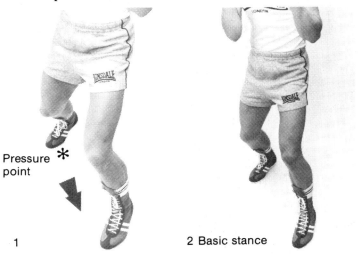

Pressure point **✱**

1

2 Basic stance

Basic footwork – pushing off the rear foot to move forward

17

Pushing off the front foot to slide the rear foot back to maintain an effective base

1 Basic stance

2 Apply pressure to ball of left foot, allowing right foot to slide back

3 Left foot slides back to resume basic stance

1

2 *

3

1

2

1 Basic stance

2 Pivoting on ball of right foot while sliding left foot forward

3 Right foot slides forward to resume basic stance

3

Moving forward and circling to the left

1

2

*

3

1 Pivoting on the ball of the front foot, sliding the rear foot back and to the right

2 Sliding front foot back into position

3 Basic stance

Moving back and circling to the right

1

2

Pushing off the front foot and sidestepping to the right

3

1 Basic stance

2 Weight on the rear foot as front foot slides backwards

3 Pressure on front foot as rear foot steps off to the right

Beginners and professionals alike should work constantly at their balance and footwork. Without this essential base, it is impossible to build the repertoire of punches and combinations.

4. The Left Jab

Most of the great champions, past and present, have relied heavily on the most basic of all punches, the left jab. This is the setting-up punch and the point scorer which can be executed from a secure defensive stance with the hand which is nearest to the opponent. There are many forms of left jab but all are related to the basic jab, the first punch

that any self-respecting coach would teach the beginner. Successful jabbing depends upon judgement of distance, timing and deception.

1. Aim for the point of the chin with the back knuckles – snap the relaxed arm away from the body, with a slight pivot at hip and shoulder.

2. The arm rotates so that the punch lands with the thumb making a small clockwise turn.

3. Slide the left foot forward before impact, and snap the hand back along the same path as the delivery.

4. The guarding hand is held high to pick off any counter-punches.

All the great names of the past – Joe Louis, Sugar Ray Robinson, Len Harvey, Randolph Turpin, Willie Pep, to name but a few – worked hard to perfect a smooth jabbing style. Use the gymnasium mirror to correct any errors in defence as the jab is snapped out.

Jabbing to the body is a skill that should not be neglected. Here, after all, is the largest part of the target area on which scoring blows can be landed. There is a two-fold advantage of jabbing to the body! Firstly as a simple points accumulator, and secondly as a means of bringing the opponent's hands down from their normal guarding position, thus exposing the chin as a further target.

When defending against jabs to the body the elbows and forearms should be used to block the punches taking care not to draw the hands away from their normal guarding positions.

Blocking and Deflecting the Jab

Little progress can be made in boxing unless the young beginner acquires a watertight defence against the jab. Initially, he will be taught to catch the opposing jab in the palm of the right hand and then he should progress to the outside parry or deflection. Here, the secret is to commit the opposing jab until it is a fraction short of the target and then with a short cuffing movement deflect the punch over the left shoulder.

Below: Deflecting or parrying the left jab

Top left: The left jab to the body

Bottom left: Blocking the jab to the body with elbows or forearms

25

Slipping and Snapping Back

The experienced professional knows full well that by slipping punches he has two free hands ready to counter. Here again, the art of slipping a punch on the outside and the inside requires constant gymnasium practice. The head, assisted by body pivot, allows the punch to slide by with a mere fraction of an inch to spare.

Slipping inside the jab

Slipping outside the jab

Snapping back to avoid the left jab. Note the wide base

The snap back can only be executed if the position of the boxer's feet affords him a large enough base. Without a sufficient base this is a dangerous move. Muhammad Ali and Tony Canzoneri were two greats who used this method of defence to enable them to snap back with a series of counter blows.

5. The Power Punches
The Straight Right

Having satisfied himself that the boxer has developed a useful left jab, and the ability to defend against the jab, the club coach will now add the power punches to the repetoire. Although it is a matter of personal preference, most coaches teach the straight right at this early stage of learning. This is a punch that should be used sparingly. It is essentially a counter-blow or a follow-up punch when the target has been opened up with the left jab. Practise the punch initially on the heavy bag, using a light left jab to measure the distance.

Again, observing the principle of pivoting around that imaginary rod or central axis, note the following points.

1. Drive off the rear foot, pivoting the hips and shoulders violently. Let the left-hand side of the body act as a hinge.

The straight right thrown at the heavy bag

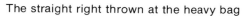

28

2. Shift the bodyweight on to the front foot, and drive the right hand fully extended at the target.

3. On impact the forearm has rotated snapping the wrist downwards, knuckles up, palm down.

4. Keep the left hand in a guarding position and see that the shoulders remain horizontal throughout the movement.

Having worked at the punch on the heavy bag, now try it on a more mobile target, such as the pads, or the palm of a partner's hand. Concentrate on moving the feet into the correct position and maintaining balance as the punch makes contact. Always aim to drive the punch two or three inches through the target. Eventually the skill will be sufficiently developed to practice in the sparring ring. Remember that, after throwing the right hand, your own target area is totally exposed to counters. With this in mind, always snap back into your normal stance after landing the punch. Eventually the good boxer develops his punches in series or combinations, and he will close his target up by throwing a left hook to complete the combination.

Defences Against the Straight Right

The good boxer should rarely be caught by a right-hand lead, as the path of the punch is in his line of vision all the way to the target. The simplest of defences, of course, is to step back out of range but this is a negative form of defence as it does not leave you in a position to counter-attack.

The Shoulder Block

This is for the beginner, a good safety-first form of defence. Here, with the feet still in punching distance, shift the weight to the back foot, turning the body sharply to the right to catch the punch high on the left shoulder. Keep the chin hidden behind this shoulder.

The shoulder block as an effective defence against powerful right-hand punches

Rolling Under the Right

This is an aggressive form of defence, a move designed to keep the opponent under constant pressure. In the face of the opposing right hand the knees dip, and the body pivots to the right to slip the head inside the punch. From this position, the head rolls under and bobs up in the outside position. The head in fact describes a 'U' shape as it bobs from 'inside' to 'out'. This move enables you to stay in a position to punch with either hand, as the opponent is now totally exposed to counters to head or body.

Straight Right to the Body

In both the amateur and professional game, powerful counter-punches to the body pay rich dividends not only as point-scoring blows, but as a means of demoralising an opponent and taking the bounce out of his legs. To score safely and effectively to the body with the right it must be thrown as a counter to a left lead or a loose right-hand lead.

1. Drop the body by bending the knees to get the shoulders in line with the target.

30

Rolling under the straight right from 'in' to 'out'

The straight right to the body

2. Keep the trunk upright and pivot the hip and shoulders to drive the right through the target.

3. At the moment of impact, the knuckles are up and the thumb is turned inward.

4. Carry the left hand in a high guarding position.

Defence Against Body Punches

Try and confine your moves to using the elbows and forearms or let your footwork take you out of range.

The Left Hook to the Chin

The left hook is perhaps the most effective punch in any champion's repertoire if it is delivered correctly. The club

coach will insist that you work long hours on the bag, and then on the pads, to learn the basic left hook. It is in the main a counter-punch and, as its name suggests, is a bent-arm blow to be used at medium and short range.

This is a difficult punch to defend against, as it is thrown from outside the main line of vision. Surprise is the key factor in its success – the opponent rarely sees it coming. The coach will use the heavy bag or pads to bring home the following points:

> 1. The weight shifts to the rear foot as the hip and shoulders pivot violently using the right side of the body as a hinge.

> 2. The left arm remains relaxed in the shape of a hook (a 90-degree angle at the elbow joint) and is whipped in an arc towards its target at the side of the chin.

Left: The left hook to the chin. Note the pivot on the ball of the front foot, and the transfer of weight to the rear foot

Right: The forearm block as a defence against the left hook

3. To enable the hips to pivot, the left foot swivels inwards on the ball of the foot.

4. At impact the knuckles point outwards, with the thumb on top.

5. Keep the right hand in a high guarding position.

The hook can now be blended into your style as an automatic counter to the opponent's left jab. First learn to wait for the opposing jab and then deflect or parry with the palm of the right glove, pivoting instantly into a sharp hooked counter to the side of the chin.

Defence

The main defences against the hook are the Forearm Block – salute with a rigid forearm, tucking the elbow in to protect the body. Better still, if you can anticipate the punch, drop the head under by bending the knees. Always keep the eyes on the opponent.

Ducking below the left hook. Don't take your eyes off your opponent

The Left Hook to the Body

This most effective punch closely resembles an uppercut, and is used on its own as a devastating counter-punch or in a combination of punches. It is aimed at the solar plexus (the point where the ribcage meets the breast-bone). The angle of delivery makes it a very difficult punch to defend against.

The left hook to the body after slipping outside the left jab

1. Slip inside or outside the jab, sliding your front foot well into range.

2. Tilt the shoulders to the left for the inside slip and over to the right when slipping outside the jab.

3. Pivot at hip and shoulder, and whip the punch steeply into the opponent's body.

4. Keep the palm of the hand facing up, and maintain a 90-degree angle at the elbow joint.

5. Exaggerate the guard with the right hand. Keep it high.

35

Defence

Avoid pulling the hands away from guarding the head and try to intercept body hooks with the elbows and forearms.

The Right Uppercut

The right uppercut is a medium- or short-range punch which demands a high degree of suppleness at the hip and shoulder joints if it is to be executed properly. A punch neglected by many boxers, the uppercut is particularly effective against short, crouching opponents. It also becomes an important punch in the repertoire of short-range blows to be used at close quarters. It is, however, as a medium-range counter-punch that the uppercut can be most devastating.

The right uppercut thrown after slipping outside the opposing jab

36

1. Taking care not to advertise the punch with a tell-tale movement of the right hand, slip inside or outside the opposing jab.

2. Tilt the weight over the right hip.

3. Rotate the hips and shoulders violently, and drive the punch up to the chin or body.

4. The palm of the hand should face up; keep the angle at the elbow joint around 90 degrees.

5. Carry the left guarding hand high.

Practise the punch on the pads or the palm of a partner's hand. Learn to throw the uppercut as you move to the left and right and as you retreat. Remember that, for a split second on launching the punch, you should be stationary and perfectly balanced.

Defence
Either step smartly out of range or block with elbows and be ready to counter sharply with your left hook.

6. Infighting
The competent boxer should master the art of fighting at long, medium and short range. If he is deficient in any of these departments, the chances of consistent success are small. When outreached by an opponent it is essential to move into close range where a wide range of short hooks and uppercuts can be used to offset the reach advantage. Over the longer distances the constant barrage of short punches to the body makes deep inroads into an opponent's stamina and invites him to lower his arms to protect the body.

Technique

1. Obtain the inside position by slipping inside the opposing jab. Carry the hands high. Try and trap the opponent in a corner or against the ropes.

2. The rear foot slides round, so that the body adopts a square-on position.

3. Taking care to keep the head up, yet around the opponent's collar bone, safely away from danger, drive the punches – short uppercuts to the body, occasionally switching to the chin – in sharp bursts with the emphasis on speed rather than power.

4. Look at your opponent through the eyebrows – a good way of keeping your chin down.

Left and above: In-fighting: two-handed
bursts of short hooks to body and head

The heavy bag can be used to practise these bursts of hooks
and uppercuts, eventually progressing to work on the pads
with your coach. The latter practice will enable you to cope
with the problem of staying close to a mobile target. When
progressing further to the sparring ring, do make sure that
you and your partner wear headguards to prevent injury
from accidentally bumped heads at this stage of learning.

7. The Southpaw

Before deciding that you wish to box as a southpaw (i.e.
right hand and right foot forward), do make sure that you
are naturally left-handed. The effective southpaw must be

particularly strong in the left leg. This is perhaps just as important as possessing a strong punch in the left hand. Too many young amateurs turn to a southpaw style, rather than adopting a style which suits them physically, because they wish to imitate a schoolboy hero. A southpaw who can only dab with his left hand, and who cannot counter off the rear foot, is easy game for the orthodox boxer. Some 40 per cent of the world's top amateurs are southpaws and these, in the main, are counter-punchers by nature and thus can cause problems unless the opponent is prepared to out-think them and beat them at their own game. In past years Lazlo Papp, Dave Charnley, Mate Parlov, Chris Finnegan and Marvin Hagler were southpaws who dominated the headlines in both the amateur and professional ranks.

8. Covering Up

There may come a phase in a fight when a boxer is faced with a two-handed attack that threatens to overwhelm him unless he resorts to covering up. Aspiring young boxers should work at the form of cover that is best suited to their own style and temperament, but they should always remember that this type of defence is only a brief temporary measure that enables the target to be protected whilst awaiting the opportunity to counter and retake the initiative. The following types of cover are worth practising until you have mastered at least two out of the three. Never take your eyes off your opponent, and be prepared to counter at the first opportunity.

Half Cover or Safety Guard

1. Shift weight to the rear foot.

2. Hide the chin behind the left shoulder.

3. The right glove is kept high, to protect the head from left hooks or swings.

4. Use the left forearm to protect the body.

Half cover or safety guard

Double Arm Cover

1. Elbows and forearms protect the body.

2. Gloves held against the cheekbones protect the chin and face.

3. Keep the body moving from the waist.

The double arm cover

41

Cross Arm Guard

This is particularly suited to the shorter boxer who is effective with his left hook, and who is likely to be subjected to uppercuts from his taller opponent.

1. Protect the chin in the crook of the right arm.

2. Use the left arm to protect the ribcage.

3. Bob and weave while looking for the opportunity to slip in a left hook counter that could turn the contest your way.

Cross arm guard

9. Basic Ringcraft
Ring Strategy

Successful ring strategy depends on the ability to out-think and outmanoeuvre the opponent in the ring; to ascertain as quickly as possible the opponent's weaknesses, strengths, and favourite attacking and defensive moves. Then to dictate the bout by using effective tactics against the opponent. Through long practice and experience, the boxer acquires the following elements of ring strategy:

42

1. Out-thinking the opposition (boxing requires brains).

2. Instantly spotting an opponent's mistake or weakness.

3. Not being too tense – it slows down the reaction time.

4. Performing basic moves well – it is the secret of success.

5. Appearing confident in the ring by avoiding any display of discomfort or tiredness.

6. Moving both anti-clockwise and clockwise; not posing.

7. Carrying the hands high at all times; keeping the chin down by watching your opponent through your eyebrows.

8. Varying the moves, by never using the same move more than twice in succession.

9. Keeping both hands punching at close quarters once the inside position is reached.

10. Never underestimating or being too impressed by an opponent.

11. Keeping on balance at all times; punching only when an opening is seen, not punching just to look busy.

12. Making sure that the bodyweight moves forward with the punch; punching with snap through the target – not at it.

13. Avoiding a right-hand lead unless an opening

exists; realising the danger of leading with wide hooks.

14. Noting the opponent's reactions or mannerisms as he leads.

15. Knowing that the safest place is in close: head above the waist, hands held high, elbows tucked in.

16. Knowing that the boxer is most vulnerable when moving into or away from an attack.

17. Knowing that the outside position is the safest place from which to launch an attack.

18. Knowing that a straight punch usually beats a hook.

19. Moving whenever the opponent gets set for a punch.

20. Never stopping trying, even when things are not going well: it takes only one well-placed punch to turn the contest around.

Ring Tactics

Ring tactics are the skills and moves used to carry out ring strategy against opponents of specific physique, style and technique.

It is difficult to generalise and evolve a blueprint that will deal with all known styles. However, the following tactics are generally regarded as the most effective:

Against a Tall Opponent
Keep moving both ways.
Draw the lead and slip inside.

Having gained the inside position, switch the attack from body to head with short hooks and uppercuts.

Against the Crouching Weaver
Do not work on a straight line.
Sidestep and work to the sides.
Punch straight and use uppercuts.

Against the Persistent Jabber
Pressure the opponent.
Weave to either side; keeping the body low, slip under the jab.
Having forced your way under the jab, punch to the body.

Against the Heavy Puncher
Keep moving – do not allow the opponent to get set.
Launch unexpected attacks.
Do not exchange punches; move away immediately.
Circle the ring in both directions.

Against the Counterpuncher
Force him to lead by feinting and drawing.
Concentrate on countering his counter.
Keep him under pressure and off balance.

Against the Southpaw
Force him to lead and make him come to you.
Circle left on to the blind side, away from the opposing left hook.
Use the left hook cross over the southpaw lead; do not neglect the right hand to head or body.

Ringcraft is the use of strategy and tactics to solve problems in the ring (it is not a substitute for physical fitness).

Boxers learn ring strategy through long experience and

practice; it depends on the ability to out-think the opponent and quickly assess his strengths and weaknesses.

Two skilful craftsmen and ring strategists. Ken Buchanan sways back from the right hand of Jim Watt, an excellent technician and, like fellow-Scot Buchanan, a former Lightweight Champion of the World.

Training for Boxing

There are few sports which make such physical demands on the competitor as boxing does. The coach will no doubt outline to would-be club members the qualities required for success in the sport at all levels. To the youngster who nevertheless takes the decision that this *is* the sport for him, the coach should point out that it will take some eight years before he can expect to reach his peak as an international amateur or a ranked professional.

It has long been accepted that you cannot acquire the physical condition needed in the modern boxing game by following the traditional methods of years gone by.

The modern coach has taken advantage of recent research into physical conditioning, and now plans his training programmes after carrying out an analysis of the necessary requirements. Any programme for the amateur or professional should be concerned with training and improving the following qualities:

1. Speed – of foot and hand movements.

2. Endurance – for the medium duration of the amateur game, and the longer times involved in professional boxing.

3. Strength – muscle power as well as endurance.

4. Joint flexibility – particularly at hip and shoulder.

47

5. A high degree of technical skill.

Basic Principles of Training
Specificity
It must be remembered that for the body to adapt to training, the conditioning required for speed, stamina and strength etc. has to be specific. Each factor requires a special type of training.

Overload
If any particular training session is to have the required effect, the intensity or the duration must exceed that which a boxer would encounter in competition. To improve his condition the boxer has to work on the principle of overload and really tax his current capacity.

Progression
To maintain any improvement gained in training, greater demands have to be made on the body progressively. Consequently training programmes have to be reviewed regularly to adjust the routines in terms of duration and intensity. This will of course be based on the needs and targets set for each individual boxer.

Regularity
Regular training is vital for the young boxer and because of the nature of the sport it is crucial that if he wishes to compete at the highest level, he should work at least five sessions in the week. The intensity and duration of the training sessions will vary accordingly but the following work cycle has proved to be a successful method for adapting the body to stress:

Day 1   Easy training
Day 2   Very hard training
Day 3   Very hard training
Day 4   Rest
Day 5   As day 1 etc.

Reversibility

When the training load is eased the bodily processes of adaptation to stress will start to drop. Thus when a high level of fitness has been achieved, the boxer cannot afford to stop working. Fitness levels soon fall away.

Rest

Many coaches maintain that rest is the most important principle of training. Heavy training sessions take a lot out of the body so rest days are vital to allow the body's systems to recover and adapt and overcompensate for the stress put upon them. Although many of the old-time trainers would have frowned at the suggestion, swimming introduced into a heavy training programme is a useful means of restoration and relaxation for the boxer.

Both the amateur and professional coach should plan the training programme with the finished product in mind, and should set goals for each year's development accordingly. Having decided the priorities for that particular year, the coach will use the following methods to bring the boxer to peak physical condition.

1. Running

To build up a reservoir of endurance there is no substitute for running, which can be introduced in a variety of forms.

1. Steady runs through woods and parkland, on roads and cross-country (flat and hilly terrain at low, medium and high speed).

2. Resistance runs as in 1. with roadwork boots or leg weights.

3. Continuous runs – starting at a relatively slow pace, accelerating gradually and finishing strongly.

4. Continuous runs – with fast starting and finishing sections and at an easy pace in the middle section.

5. Continuous runs – with pace acceleration uphill and medium to all-out effort.

6. Continuous runs – with fixed alternation between low and medium speed, low and high speed, medium and high speed over middle and long distances.

7. Fartlek (speed play) – running an optional total distance with easy and fast sections.

8. Cross-country – identical with continuous running, but over difficult changing ground mainly at average high speed. This type of run requires willpower. Variations underfoot and changes in the level of the ground develop strength and endurance in the legs.

Having laid down a platform of general, heart and lung endurance, the boxer has, of course, to train the body to adapt to the stress that he is likely to encounter in a hard fight, whether it be over three rounds or fifteen. For much of the time in a contest he will be able to box within himself without having to sustain a very high pulse rate, i.e. the body is said to be working in a 'steady state'. However, to increase the volume of work and step up the pace it is essential that at some time in his training routine he uses the 'interval method' of running. Here he subjects the heart and lung system to repeated doses of stress, while working at about 80 per cent maximum effort. Various researchers have found that the maximum training effect was obtained when the pulse rate at the end of a run was around 180 beats per minute and then allowed to recover to between 140 and 120 beats before repeating the run. For amateurs involved in three-round bouts the most effective results were obtained by running distances that did not exceed 400 metres.

Clothing and Footwear for Running

As the competition season for boxing is in the winter months, it is important to wrap up warmly in sweat suit or tracksuit. As the head is the first part of the body to cool off after sweating, a hooded training top should also be worn. The choice of footwear will depend on the type of running. For steady mileage work, roadwork boots can be worn and for interval and speed work, training shoes are ideal. To prevent blistering, *woollen* socks are recommended.

The Use of the Pulse Rate in Training

Although it would be wrong for coaches to be obsessive about pulse rate, perhaps the following points will act as a guide. The beat of the heart may be felt as a pulsation in a number of arteries of the body. The pulse may be detected in the radial artery at the wrist and in the carotid artery in the neck. At rest in the average adult, the pulse rate would be 70 beats per minute. In trained athletes it is slower and a rate of 50-60 beats per minute is common. It is not unusual to record rates of 40 beats per minute in the highly-trained endurance athlete. 'Homicide' Henry Armstrong, the triple world champion of the late 1930s, was known to have an abnormally low resting pulse rate of around 35 beats per minute.

(There are many factors other than exercise affecting the

Above, right and over page: former World Champion Terry Marsh jogging, striding and sprinting, aspects of running vital to all boxers' training routines

heart rate: a new-born baby's heart beats 130 times per minute, gradually reducing to 70 beats per minute in the adult, women's hearts beat between 5 and 10 beats per minute faster than men's, changing from the lying to the standing position can increase the heart rate by 10 beats per minute, and an increased heart rate occurs during digestion, highly emotional excitement, high body

temperature (fever), high external temperature, anaemia and smoking.)

An increase in pulse rate occurs immediately before the exercise begins. Thereafter, there is a rapid rise to the maximum rate required for the workload. Amateur boxers record high pulse rates, whereas professionals, working

54

over a longer distance, produce a much lower peak heart rate. At the end of the particular workload there is a rapid fall in the pulse rate, which then levels off for a time before gradually returning to normal. There are marked individual variations among trained boxers. It is of value to know the pulse rate for a particular work-out as additional evidence of performance, but rigid reliance on the pulse rate as a guide to interval training should be avoided. Random checks should be sufficient. The coach who knows his boxer well, and uses a stop watch regularly, will find that the pulse rate is best used as back-up evidence of performance.

Schedule of Intensive Interval Running for Amateur and Professional Boxers

Distance	Running Speed (Approx.)	Recovery Period Jogging/Walking	Number of Repetitions (Approx.)
Novices and Juniors (14-16 years)			
100 m	20-17 secs.	100-60 secs.	8-10
200 m	42-38 secs.	120-90 secs.	6-8
300 m	60-54 secs.	130-90 secs.	5-7
400m	100-80 secs.	150-90 secs.	4-6
Amateur Boxers (17+ years)			
100 m	16-14 secs.	90-60 secs.	10-12
200 m	36-32 secs.	120-60 secs.	8-10
300 m	56-52 secs.	120-90 secs.	6-8
400 m	90-70 secs.	150-120 secs.	6-8
Professional Boxers			
100 m	15-14 secs.	60-45 secs.	10-12
200 m	33-29 secs.	90-45 secs.	8-10
300 m	58-48 secs.	90-45 secs.	8-10
400 m	72-60 secs.	120-60 secs.	6-8
500 m	110-80 secs.	120-60 secs.	6-8
600 m	130-110 secs.	180-90 secs.	4-6
800 m	160-140 secs.	180-90 secs.	4-6
1,000 m	205-180 secs.	300-120 secs.	4-6

Although it is more convenient to use a track for ease of measurement and timing, it is by no means essential. Fields and areas of common land can be used with equal success. Pavements and lamp-posts have been used for years for the same purpose, but perhaps for training of lesser intensity.

As speed is also an essential ingredient in the boxer's make-up, time should be taken to include shuttle sprints over distances up to 60m particularly in the final preparation stages before the fight or competition.

2. Warm-up and Flexibility Work

There is no doubt that a boxer's skills and performance in training and in the ring are greatly affected by warm-up or lack of it. Physiologically, a warm-up means that an adequate supply of blood is present in the required muscles at the start of the fight or training session. A warm muscle contracts more speedily than a cold one. The warm-up should be related to the job in hand but, at the same time, for punches to be thrown efficiently, the hip and shoulder joints should be stretched through the full range of the joint using a series of stretching exercises. However, the body should be warmed thoroughly first by jogging and light shadow boxing before the gradual stretching movements begin.

A warm-up session of 10-15 minutes is essential before any heavy training session. Likewise, after a heavy session, 'warm-down' for 10 minutes with light jogging and stretching exercises to eliminate the build-up of waste products that cause stiffness in the muscles.

Stretching Exercises

All stretching exercises should be done slowly, without any

56

Stretching exercises: starting
with the neck area, and
working down through the
body

bouncing movement. Stretch to where you feel a slight
tension in the muscle and joint. Hold this feeling for 5 to 30
seconds. As you hold this stretch, the feeling of tension
should diminish. This easy stretch prepares the tissues for
further stretching and increasing suppleness.

57

Stretching at the shoulder joint
and the oblique muscles of the
trunk

Back, trunk and hamstring
stretching exercises

Stretching exercises for the back, thighs, hip joint and trunk

60

After holding the easy stretch, move a fraction of an inch further into the stretch until mild tension is felt again. This is the 'development' stretch which should again be held for 5 to 30 seconds. If the tension increases and becomes painful, ease off back to a comfortable stretch. This development stretch is designed to reduce tension in the muscles and increase flexibility in the joints.

Hold only the stretch tensions that feel good to you. Be relaxed as you concentrate on the area being stretched. Breathe deeply and slowly.

This type of gradual stretching routine is a vital part of a boxer's warm-up.

3. Speed
This is mainly dependent on the strength of the prime mover muscles and the type of actual muscle fibres. Recent research has shown conclusively that there are two types of muscle fibre: fast twitch, responsible for explosive movement, and slow twitch, which lends itself to endurance-type activity but not to speed. The ratio of fast twitch fibres to slow twitch in the muscular make-up of any particular boxer will decide his effectiveness in his chosen sport, and will explain why some individuals are slow off the mark while others appear to have a natural speed of movement.

No matter which type the performer belongs to, flexibility exercises and constant practice of the skills at maximum speed will ensure that each boxer will attain his individual maximum speed of movement.

Both amateurs and professionals should consciously work

Johnny Clark, former European Bantamweight Champion,
working out with the speedball

at speed of hand and foot in the gymnasium. Keep the
movements in shadow boxing and bag work sharp and
avoid sloppy moves that can easily develop into faulty

Spar pads: favoured by many
coaches when working to perfect
a boxer's technique

techniques. Work on the speedball and pads, geared to snap shots and sharp combinations, will assist in the maintenance of speed of hand movements. While working on the speedball, do not neglect to move the feet.

Tony Sibson, former British and European Middleweight Champion, throwing sharp combinations on the pads

4. Strength
Circuit Training

Perhaps the most important form of strength required by a boxer is muscular endurance; the ability to repeatedly contract and relax the muscles in the arms, trunk and legs without fatigue setting in. The training of this fitness factor is vital to the boxer and is a process built up gradually over the years by a system of progressively overloading the

Press-up:
hold body in
straight line,
extend arms
fully

Sit-up with
twist: hold
twist all way
up and down

Shuttle runs:
touch floor
with hands

64

Dorsal raise:
hands behind
neck

Squat jump
with dumb-
bells:
alternate feet
forward

Wrestler's
bridge: roll
from crown
to forehead

Left, above and over page: The suggested
exercises for a suitable muscular and general
endurance circuit

65

Dumb-bell
punching

Star jump

Pike sit-up

Dorsal raise:
arms extended

66

muscle groups. Experience shows that rapidly acquired strength, speed and endurance are lost more quickly than those gained during a long and constantly intensified training programme.

In most sports, circuit training has been accepted as an ideal training method that will improve both muscular endurance and general endurance (stamina). Performed properly, this kind of training also gives a fair indication of the resolve and determination of the boxer involved. Circuit training can take many forms, but all methods should motivate each boxer to work to the maximum of his own ability. Circuits can be adjusted to suit whatever number of rounds you are training for, but care should be taken to change the exercises regularly – muscles cease to gain in strength unless there is a change in stimulus.

A useful form of circuit that can be used by the amateur or professional is the 'fixed load' circuit. As in all forms of circuit training, large numbers can be accommodated but each works at his own level of performance. Here the coach lays down three circuits of increasing intensity and prescribes the training dose (number of repetitions) for each activity. Thus, one boxer might be working on the yellow circuit, one on the red and one on the blue. On each colour circuit there is an overall target time for three laps. When the boxer is consistently beating the target time for the three laps, he is promoted to the next colour circuit. The training dose can be printed on large coloured cards at each activity, e.g. sit-ups: yellow – 12; red – 16; blue – 20. It is usual to increase the number of repetitions by about one third.

To maintain the progressive overload principle, and

67

varying the exercise to stimulate the muscle groups, load the activities with appropriate weights.

Suggested Circuit for Muscular and General Endurance

Target Times for 3 Laps*: Blue-18 minutes; Red-20 minutes; Yellow-22 minutes

1. Press-ups	B – 20	6. Wrestler's bridge	B – 20
	R – 16		R – 14
	Y – 12		Y – 10
2. Sit-ups (inclined bench)	B – 20 R – 16 Y – 12	7. Dumb-bell punching (vary weights 1-5lb)	B – 50 R – 40 Y – 30
3. Shuttle run (10 metres)	B – 10 R – 8 Y – 6	8. Pike sit-ups	B – 20 R – 16 Y – 12
4. Dorsal raise (hands behind neck)	B – 20 R – 16 Y – 12	9. Burpee jumps	B – 20 R – 16 Y – 12
5. Squat jumps (with weights)	B – 20 R – 16 Y – 12	10. Dorsal raise (arms extended)	B – 20 R – 16 Y – 12

* For beginners, the target times should be adjusted to *two* laps. In the early stages it is advisable to allow a one-minute rest between laps.

Variety is, of course, all-important in strength training. The following types of circuit training can be incorporated into the programme:

The Target Circuit

Here the exercises are specified by the coach, but the boxer does not have a limited number to complete. His aim is to 'score' as many repetitions as possible in the given time (which is usually between thirty and sixty seconds). No rest is given between exercises, although it may be unavoidable if boxers have to move from one area of the gym to another.

For boxers the following is an interesting and worthwhile use of this method, and very strenuous. No expensive equipment is necessary.

Select six activities from the list bearing in mind the muscle groups involved in each activity.

The boxer spends thirty seconds working flat out on the first activity, then on the whistle or shout moves immediately to the second activity, etc. A running total is kept on all activities. A one-minute rest is allowed – this recovery period can be cut down – and the circuit is completed a second and a third time. This attempts to represent the duration and workload of a three-round contest, and can be increased for those involved with a longer distance. Although the number of activities *can* be increased from six, the stress imposed by 30 seconds of work at each may be too severe, so that it may be necessary to reduce the time at each activity to 20 seconds to obtain a useful workload without the boxer breaking down. If the target for each activity drops below 15 seconds, the training effect becomes minimal.

Circuits in Well-equipped Gymnasia

For clubs lucky enough to use a school or technical college

69

gymnasium, the activities can be made more interesting and the following list should be of some assistance in laying out an effective circuit:

1. Rope climb, arms only.

2. Double rope swing to touch high beam with feet.

3. Sit-ups on inclined bench.

4. Pull-overs on inclined bench.

5. Bench lifts.

6. Step-ups on double bench.

7. Bench jumps holding weights.

8. Split jumps with weights.

The following need weights or resistance of some form:

1. Triceps pull.

2. Alternate arm press.

3. Lateral bent arm raise.

Ton-up Circuits

Here we select 10 exercises that do not require apparatus, and perform 10 'quality' repetitions of each. This circuit can be repeated two or three times depending upon the intensity of the training session. This circuit can be arduous if the exercises selected enable the boxer to work against his own bodyweight. During the close season phase they add variety to other strength sessions and make an ideal finish to a 'Fartlek' run.

Some suggested exercises:

1. Push-ups – alternate leg raising.
2. 'V' sit-ups.
3. Dorsal raise – arms extended.
4. Squat jumps.
5. Bounce push-ups.
6. Bent knee sit-ups.
7. Dorsal raise – hands behind neck.
8. Pike jumps – with split.
9. Snake push-ups.
10. Wrestler's bridge.

Improvement is gauged by the time taken to complete the circuit. Ideal when working with groups of 10 or more.

Bar or beam activities: chins – undergrasp, overgrasp, behind neck. Pull-ups and mount. Leg circling.

There is little doubt that enormous benefit could be obtained if circuit training became a regular part of a boxer's training programme, particularly as an early season basis for general fitness training. For in-season work, too, many clubs have found a keen response from boys who can now see the improvement in their level of fitness.

When planning a boxer's yearly programme, the various types of circuit training are introduced to suit the type of work required at each particular point in the season. It is also vital that changes of circuit are made to add variety and new stimuli to the training routine.

Safety Tips for Trainers

1. Make sure that the type and intensity of the circuit is suitable for the age and physical maturity of the boxer.

2. Warm up thoroughly first and make sure that all concerned are familiar with the exercise. Keep the movements as simple as possible if athletes are working under stress.

3. Check all weights and apparatus for safety defects: e.g., loose collars on weights and broken balancing benches.

4. Avoid crowding at each exercise station by organising the work carefully.

5. Ensure boxers 'warm-down' thoroughly for 10 minutes after each session.

Weight Training

N.B. It is not recommended that boys under 14 years start training with weights.

Since the Germans first used a systematic weight-training scheme to prepare their athletes for the 1936 Olympic Games, the use of this method of strength training has become the rule rather than the exception. Boxing coaches, however, have been reluctant to abandon age-old 'groundwork' methods, despite the fact that all available research on the subject of muscular strength has long since dismissed these archaic systems.

The boxer's armoury of fitness must include heart-lung endurance, power, local muscular endurance, flexibility

72

and a high degree of technical skill. The development of strength at the expense of the other factors will leave rather obvious loopholes in a boxer's preparation, and from the outset one should be aware of the limitations of weight training as well as the advantages.

There are three main areas in the overall development programme of the aspiring international boxer which are catered for by a carefully-planned weight training (or progressive resistance training) programme.

1. As part of a general build-up of fitness and endurance as related specifically to a rugged combat sport, and to assist in the rapid recovery from the bumps and stresses of the event – the 'tolerance to punishment' factor.

2. To develop power (strength $\times$ speed) of punch, and the ability to perform the skills of attack and defence which also require power. To acquire also the local muscular endurance without which many of boxing's complex skills break down.

3. By the developing and strengthening of muscle over its full range of movement, thus ensuring greater flexibility in the joints essential for the smooth, skilled performance of the top-class boxer. This is an essential part of any fitness programme.

In preparing a programme of progressive resistance exercises for an 'athlete', it is important to have these fundamental objectives clear in one's mind. Obviously, the type of weight-training programme for the heavy field athlete will differ considerably from that to be employed by the amateur boxer. With a carefully-planned programme, therefore, we can expect to produce several end results. These are:

1. Fitness of a general nature.
2. Specific muscle endurance.
3. Overall general strength.
4. Speed.
5. Power.

Cardio-vascular Fitness

Although there can be no substitute for running in a boxer's training routine, weight training can also be designed to assist the general fitness build-up. The type of exercises used in the fitness programme are those which employ large groups of muscles at one time. The object is to place great overload on the cardio-vascular system – such exercises would include power cleaning and snatching, high pull-ups, squats, lunges and bench-pressing. All these exercises are of a massive nature.

The repetitions must be high. A resistance is chosen that will permit ten repetitions without the loss of form. As the 'athlete' finds it easier to perform the ten repetitions, so he progresses to fifteen and from there to twenty in easy stages. When the selected maximum is achieved, the weight is increased so that he can now only perform ten repetitions again. The process is then repeated until he reaches the required maximum.

Rest pauses between sets of repetitions and between

74

exercises should be kept to the minimum. These pauses should only be long enough to permit the breathing to return to a level which will not affect the skill or rhythm of the movement. In actual time this is usually between 30 and 90 seconds, depending on the number of repetitions and the resistance used.

Endurance

Endurance training is an extension of fitness work. The repetitions can be increased considerably up to as many as 50. The exercise chosen should again be of a massive nature involving large muscle groups, and the weights used should be light with the high repetitions performed at speed. The rest pauses between sets should be as short as possible.

Strength and Power Training

When we train for strength and power we adopt the opposite procedure to that employed in Fitness and Endurance training. There is now a need to use a much heavier resistance, with consequently lower repetitions. The resistance selected should not permit more than five repetitions to be performed for any exercise and the total number of repetitions should not exceed 25. At times it may be necessary to handle weights which permit only three or two repetitions and the 'athlete' may well go to singles where maximum resistance is being handled. Good power exercises would include – high pull-ups, power cleans, power snatch, upward jumps, heave presses and jerks with barbells and dumb-bells.

Speed

Successful speed training is dependent on increases in

strength and power. Nevertheless, all exercises for the boxer must be performed with a conscious effort for more speed in the movement. It must be stressed that a boxer must never lose sight of this factor in his preparation.

Planning the Programme

Although international commitments spread over the calendar make efforts to plan for peak performance very difficult, it is now becoming more widely accepted in boxing that the year must be programmed in the same manner that the year of track and field athletics is tackled. The programme can therefore be divided into the following sections:

1. Close season.

2. Pre-season phase.

3. Early season.

4. Competitive season.

1. Close Season

The best time to introduce weight-training to the boxer is during the close or non-competitive phase of the season. This will give the coach the opportunity to follow a comprehensive schedule concerned with laying down the platform of hard-core fitness, flexibility and strength on which he can build as the season progresses. The schedule will be general, employing exercises for all muscle groups. The repetitions will be high so that adequate stress will be placed on the cardio-vascular system and the resistance principle will be directed primarily to the increase of repetitions. This period should last from three to six weeks, with three training sessions per week. To begin with, the boxer should use weights that he can handle easily but towards the end of the period, the coach should have a good idea of the weight that his man can work with in the subsequent phases of training.

2. Pre-Season Phase

For some four to eight weeks prior to the start of the season, the number of exercises will be cut down and those of a massive nature employed. The resistance is increased with a corresponding reduction in the number of repetitions. The set system is now used, with the major aim being an increase in power. Again, the training should consist of three sessions per week leading into the next phase.

3. Early Season

During this period, for about four weeks, a schedule directed to power building should be employed. Again the exercises are of a massive nature, but now attempts can be made at maximums. This means that an exercise can be followed on a pyramid repetition basis (e.g., 5 reps $\times$ 40lbs, 4 reps $\times$ 50lbs, 3 reps $\times$ 60lbs, 2 reps $\times$ 70lbs, 1 rep $\times$ 80lbs, 1 rep $\times$ 80lbs).

When a number of sets and repetitions is decided upon, then there can be an increase in the poundage handled in each set. When the season has begun and the demands of competition increase, this period and the subsequent phase will involve two sessions per week only.

4. Peak Competitive Season

Once the competition season is intensive, the object of

training becomes one of maintenance. With this in mind, the power developed in the earlier periods can be maintained with two sessions per week. It is important from both a psychological and physiological point of view to avoid a dull routine. Thus two separate schedules can be followed during this phase to avoid boredom and to allow the body to adapt to a change in training stimulus. Select good general power exercises and a resistance sufficient to ensure that the repetitions are kept low. Perform five sets of each exercise. Since the use of weights is challenging in itself, do not be afraid to let the boxer increase the poundage that he can handle provided that he does not lose sight of speed and maintains the correct lifting technique at all times.

If there is any doubt in the coach's or boxer's mind about weight training, contact should be made with any British Amateur Weight Lifters' Association qualified coach who will be able to offer advice on safe lifting techniques and the programme you are attempting. If there is difficulty in locating a suitable coach in your area, contact the B.A.W.L.A. Honorary Secretary at 3 Iffley Turn, Oxford.

In conclusion, it is worth noting the words of an eminent American athletic coach and authority on weight training:

> 'There is no short cut to strength development, as there is none for the development of skill, agility, or endurance in an athlete. No amount of fancy gimmicks or equipment or adoption of alleged time-saving "fads" will substitute for a long-term pro-gramme of hard work, that is required to develop the quality of strength needed by an athlete for optimum performance in his speciality. Greater progress in

track and field performances during the past fifteen years has been the result of harder work by athletes, not by resorting to short cuts and less work.'

Safety Precautions

1. Warm-up and warm-down before and after each session.

2. Master the lifting techniques with a lighter load.

3. Stand close to the bar and lift with a flat straight back.

4. Breathe in with the greatest effort and out when the weight is lowered. The reverse is true when doing squats or sit-ups.

5. Check the collars on the bars after loading.

Weight Training Exercises for the Mature Boxer

Starting position

WEIGHT TRAINING PR(
PHYSICALL

<table>
<tr><th colspan="3" align="center">CLOSE SEASON</th><th colspan="3" align="center">PRE-SEASON</th></tr>
<tr>
<td colspan="3" align="center">Hard-core fitness work. Flexibility
High pulse rate–Short rest</td>
<td colspan="3" align="center">Strength build-up</td>
</tr>
<tr>
<td colspan="3" align="center">3 times per week</td>
<td colspan="3" align="center">3 times per week</td>
</tr>
<tr>
<td colspan="3" align="center">Mon.   Wed.   Fri.</td>
<td colspan="3" align="center">Mon.   Wed.   Fri.</td>
</tr>
<tr><td></td><td>Set</td><td>Reps</td><td></td><td>Sets</td><td>Reps</td></tr>
<tr><td>High pull-up</td><td>1</td><td>10-20</td><td>Power cleans</td><td>4</td><td>8</td></tr>
<tr><td>Press behind neck</td><td>1</td><td>10-20</td><td>Bench press</td><td>4</td><td>8</td></tr>
<tr><td>Two hands curl</td><td>1</td><td>10-20</td><td>Back squats</td><td>4</td><td>8</td></tr>
<tr><td>D/B side bend</td><td>1</td><td>10-20</td><td>D/B two-handed</td><td></td><td></td></tr>
<tr><td>Bent-forward rowing</td><td>1</td><td>10-20</td><td> lateral punch</td><td>4</td><td>8</td></tr>
<tr><td>Back squat</td><td>1</td><td>10-20</td><td>Split squats</td><td>4</td><td>10</td></tr>
<tr><td>Power cleans</td><td>1</td><td>10-20</td><td>Abdominals (sit-ups</td><td></td><td></td></tr>
<tr><td>Bench press</td><td>1</td><td>10-20</td><td> with weight)</td><td>4</td><td>10</td></tr>
<tr><td>Pull overs (straight arm)</td><td>1</td><td>10-20</td><td>Wrestler's bridge</td><td></td><td></td></tr>
<tr><td>Abdominals (sit-ups)</td><td>1</td><td>10-30</td><td> (Face down)</td><td>2</td><td>10</td></tr>
<tr><td>Neck exercise</td><td>1</td><td>10-20</td><td>Wrestler's bridge</td><td></td><td></td></tr>
<tr><td> (Wrestler's bridge,
  face up)</td><td></td><td></td><td> (Face up)</td><td>2</td><td>10</td></tr>
</table>

WARM-UP AND WARM-DOWN before and after each session

GRAMME FOR THE
MATURE BOXER

*3-6 weeks depending on
existing level of fitness*
EARLY SEASON

Power build-up

2 times per week

Mon.	*Wed.*		
		Set	Reps
Power cleans		5-4-3	2-1-1
Bench press		5-4-3	2-1-1
Squat jumps		3	5
Alt. arm press D/B		3	5
Side bends		2	8
Abdominals (bent knee sit-up with twist)		2	8
Wrestler's bridge (Face up)		2	8
Wrestler's bridge (Face down)		2	8

4 weeks

Power maintenance

2 times per week

	Sets	Reps
Schedule 'A' Monday		
Power cleans	5	4
Bench press	5	4
D/B two-handed lateral punch	5	4
Split squats	5	6
Abdominals (bent knee sit-up with twist)	5	6
Wrestler's bridge (Face up)	5	6
Schedule 'B' Wednesday		
High pulls (wide grip)	5	4
Squat jumps	5	4
Power cleans	5	4
Split squats (each leg)	5	6
D/B punching (each arm)	5	6
Wrestler's bridge (face down)	5	6

*Remainder of competitive
season*

High pull up

Curls

Back squat

Bench press

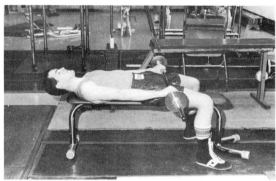

aight arm pull over: 1

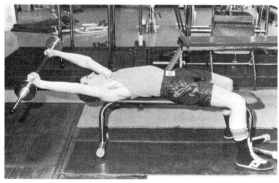

Straight arm pull over: 2

83

Press behind neck   Press behind neck

Side bends

84

Bent forward rowing

Bend forward rowing

Power clean

Power clean

Two-handed lateral punch   Split squats

Bent knee sit ups

Wrestler's bridge

86

Wrestler's bridge

Alternate arm press

Squat jump   Squat jump

Work in the Gymnasium

The gym is the boxer's workshop, and there he must learn and master the skills of the game and condition his body for the stress of competition.

Equipment: each boxer should be urged to supply his own personal training gear. As a novice amateur he could probably expect the club to supply spar gloves, bag gloves and skipping ropes, but having committed himself to taking the sport seriously he should take pride in his appearance both in the gym and in the competition ring. Here are the essential items that should be packed in his training bag.

    Personal headguard
    Towelling gown
    Jockstrap
    Towel
    Track training shoes and boxing boots
    Trunks
    Skipping rope
    Sparring gloves – 12 or 14oz., depending on fighting
        weight
    Punchbag gloves
    Socks
    Foulproof protector
    Personally-fitted gumshield
    Bandages

Adhesive tape
Clean training T-shirt
Shower sandals

All boxers should be encouraged to use their own sparring gloves as the variation in the size of hands tends to disrupt the padding in 'club' gloves. This can, of course, lead to incorrect punching. The gumshield is a vital piece of equipment for cushioning the effect of blows and preventing chipped teeth and lacerations inside the mouth. Bandages, of course, should always be worn in the gymnasium.

Sparring

The training ring is a place for sharpening skills, where headguards, sparring gloves and gumshields should always be worn and the coach should be in complete control to ensure that the boxers are learning as they work. Apart from the spar that sharpens the skills for a specific fight, coaches should also use a 'conditioned' spar where both boxers work to set orders in order to develop a particular move or skill. A further form of spar used in East European countries is the 'technique' spar, with the emphasis on speed and balance; the punches are thrown at the palm of the guarding hand and the forearms. Again this is a valuable exercise, especially in the early learning stages.

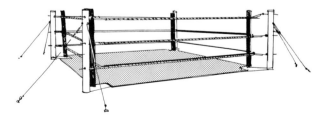

Shadow Boxing

A mirror used sensibly is a useful training aid and enables the boxer to check his stance and spot loopholes in his defence. When shadow boxing, concentrate all the time and use your imagination to envisage an opponent in front of you. Little purpose is served by snorting and moving the shoulders in the imitation of punches – rather, punch sharply without overreaching the arms and risking damage at the elbow joint. Never work with the mouth open, always try to breathe through the nose. The jaw is most susceptible to injury if struck when the teeth are not clenched.

Using the Gym Equipment
Punchbags

The bag is used by the champion and novice alike to develop and sharpen their repertoire of punches. The bag can be used to increase leverage and to build up the

numbers of punches in the various combinations. Floyd Patterson, under his mentor Cus D'Amato, built up a bewildering series of punches by working diligently on the heavy bag. At one stage both he and Jose Torres, the former World Light Heavyweight Champion, worked on punchbags with various combinations numbered and marked on the bag. In this way, the patterns of muscular movement become instinctive so that, on a given cue, the boxer responds with a fast burst of predetermined punches. Always wear bandages and your own personal bag gloves.

Punch Pads

The pads are a vital coaching aid and can also be used as a means of putting pressure on the boxer during a training round. The pads are also used as a progression from bag work where patterns of punching can be perfected on a moving target. The coach may find it a useful exercise on occasions to wear one pad and one glove on the leading hand used to produce a variety of counters against a left or right lead. Finally, the pads can be used to develop speed and sharpness as the coach proffers them for snap shots or quick bursts from hidden positions behind his back.

Weighted bag gloves: used to build arm and shoulder power

Wall Bags

Very popular in Eastern Europe and useful for developing combinations of straight-arm punches. They may also be used for stamina training when used for sustained bursts of punching on the interval training principle.

Speed Ball

When used properly, the speed ball develops a degree of muscular endurance in the arms and shoulders. Always remember to use the feet in co-ordination with the hands. Aside from the steady rhythm of punching, try to fire in a series of quick combinations to sharpen up the timing and co-ordination.

Maize Ball

A useful bag used to develop speed and timing combined with footwork. Ingemar Johansson popularised this simple piece of equipment which he used to develop his lightning 'one two' combination which won him the World Heavyweight Title from Floyd Patterson in 1959.

Floor-to-Ceiling Ball

Provided that it is attached safely, this is a ball which can be

Tony Sibson
sharpening up on
the floor-to-ceiling
ball

used to develop a fine sense of timing and co-ordination as
the boxer works both in an anti-clockwise and clockwise
direction. It is also useful to practise counter-punches as
you lay back with the weight on the back foot.

Stand Ball

A useful piece of equipment for the beginner. (Note the
particularly solid base on this Lonsdale ball, which can be
bolted to the gym floor.)

Former World
Champion
Terry Marsh
showing a
variety of
skipping methods

94

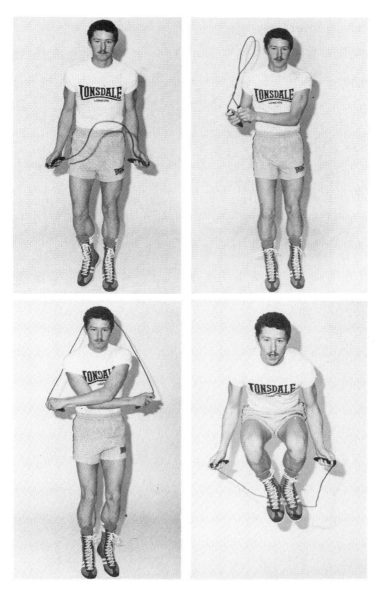

Skipping Rope

The skipping rope is very much a personal item of equipment adjusted to your own height. Leather ropes are recommended, but the junior boxer may find the plastic version more suited to his pocket. The rope can be used for 'steady state' endurance work, or used for developing speed in short, sharp bursts on the interval training principle, with the rest period geared accordingly. The beginner should persevere with his rope skipping as he will eventually progress to the more advanced skills of rope crossing and double jumping. To encourage a sense of rhythm, many of the great champions of the past, including 'Sugar' Ray Robinson, skipped to lively beat music.

Medicine Ball

Add a little variety to your strengthening routines by using a medicine ball. Here are some exercises calculated to work on the arms and the upper body. Particular emphasis is placed on the back and the oblique muscles of the trunk. Try them in two sets of eight repetitions building up gradually to three sets of twelve repetitions.

 Medicine ball exercises

97

A selection of exercises designed to add a little variety to the strength training programme

98

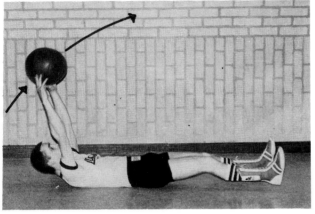

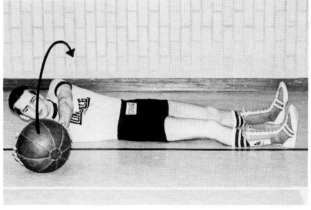

101

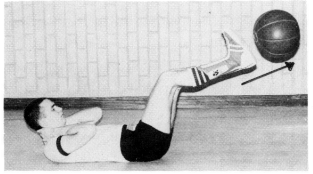

102

Work in the Corner

In the gymnasium, the coach's working uniform should be a track suit. He should set a good example in attitude and appearance. A slipshod appearance tends to reflect defective coaching methods. It is even more important that when he is appearing before the public, in a boxer's corner, he should present a good image. The sport, both the amateur and professional codes, is not without its critics

Bobby Neil, former trainer of World Champions Alan Minter and Lloyd Honeyghan wearing the essential second's jacket and armed with ice bag and water bottle

and defensive claims of self-discipline and sportsmanship count for nothing if the behaviour of boxer and seconds in the ring do not reflect these virtues. Working in the corner requires the chief second not only to be a good 'reader' of a fight and a good motivator, but also a good first aid and repair man. As the second must be able to lay his hands on a variety of items from scissors to swab sticks, a second's jacket, with its numerous pockets for his all-important repair equipment, is an important garment.

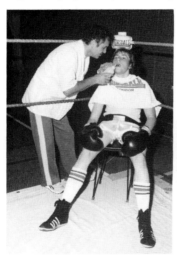
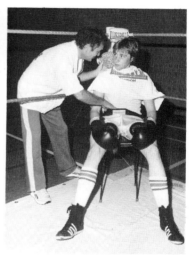

Good corner work. The boxer is seated comfortably with hands in lap before the coach offers a drink of water or any form of advice

104

Getting Ready for the Contest
Bandaging

Both amateurs and professionals should take great care over the preparation of their hands for a contest. The human hand was made for grasping rather than punching and there is a need to protect the fine bones forming the back of the hand (metacarpals) from spreading on impact. The thumb also needs some protection as well as support for the wrist. The amateur tends to use crepe or cotton velpeau bandage but may use only a small strip of adhesive plaster at the wrist. Many amateurs like to bandage their own hands after initial guidance from their coach.

Bandaging the Hands for Amateur Boxing

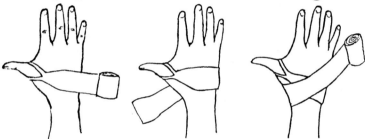

1 Starting position. 2 To the base of thumb. 3 To big knuckle of little finger.

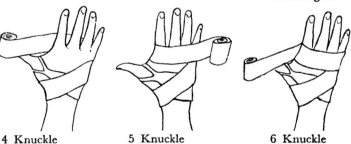

4 Knuckle encirclement.　　5 Knuckle encirclement.　　6 Knuckle encirclement.

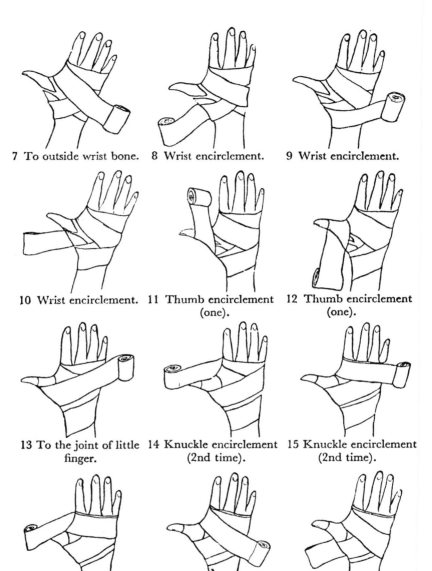

7 To outside wrist bone. 8 Wrist encirclement. 9 Wrist encirclement.

10 Wrist encirclement. 11 Thumb encirclement (one). 12 Thumb encirclement (one).

13 To the joint of little finger. 14 Knuckle encirclement (2nd time). 15 Knuckle encirclement (2nd time).

16 Knuckle encirclement (2nd time). 17 Diagonally across back of hand. 18 To base of thumb.

106

19 Thumb encirclement (2nd time).   20 Thumb encirclement (2nd time).

21 To wrist.   22 Wrist encirclement and tape.

Crepe bandages must be applied carefully as there is a tendency for the elastic to tighten, thus hindering the circulation in the hand. Make sure also that they are not damp or creased. Roll them carefully before putting them away in your bag after use.

Bandaging the Hands for Professional Boxing

The professional fighter's livelihood depends very often on the condition of his hands so it is usual for his chief second to apply the tape and bandage (both soft bandage and gauze) according to B.B.B. of C. regulations.

Board of Control Rules state that the length of 2-inch soft bandage on each hand should not exceed 18 feet for all

107

weights. In addition 9 feet of 1-inch zinc oxide plaster may be used for weights up to middleweight; for light-heavy and heavyweights 11 feet is permissible.

The following method, outlined by Bill Chevalley, coach of former British Middleweight Champion, Mark Rowe, is generally accepted as standard in professional boxing.

Bandaging

(Fig. a) Hold the hand at a comfortable height, with the thumb towards the chest and fingers loosely spread. Using 2-inch cotton or linen bandage start at the wrist and work towards the little finger, protect the wrist and thumb with two or three turns around the base of the thumb joint and wrist.

(Fig. b) Keeping the hand in the same position, cross the bandage at the back of the hand, around the palm and bring the bandage back to the base of the first finger.

(Figs. c and d) Take the bandage across the knuckles. Lap the bandage to and fro to give added protection to the knuckles. Holding the lapped bandage in position, bandage completely around the palm and knuckles, crossing the bandage at the back of the hand and around the wrist. Try making a fist so that the bandage fits comfortably until the roll runs out. Finish at the wrist and seal the bandage with a strip of tape.

(Fig. e) The finished hand clenched for punching.

Taping

(Figs. f, g and h) To give additional support to the small bones of the hand, in professional boxing, taping is allowed.

108

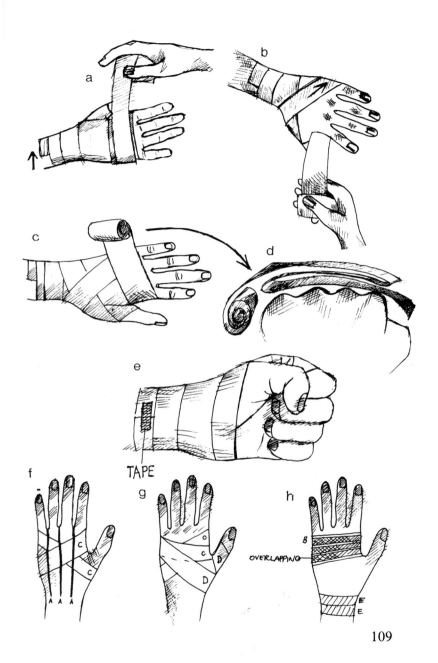

a

b

c

d

e

TAPE

f

g

h

C

C

A A A

D

C

D

B

OVERLAPPING

E
E

109

Using 1-inch surgical tape (obtainable from Lonsdale in a large roll), tear off or cut:

(a) 1 strip $\frac{7}{8}$ inch, then snip into three equal strips.

(b) 4 strips 5 inches long.

(c) 1 strip 10 inches long.

(d) 8 strips the width of the hand.

(e) 1 strip to encircle the wrist twice.

After bandaging the hands apply the three smallest strips (a) between the fingers on the palm and the back of the hand. Make a fist, lifting the strips of tape to tighten in this position.

Place four strips 5 inches long (b) in the following positions:

1. With the fist clenched, two strips criss-crossed at the back of the hand, making sure the base of the thumb is protected.

2. A third piece of tape is taken diagonally across the palm to the base of the thumb. A fourth piece is stretched across the palm from the wrist to the base of the first finger.

Take a 10-inch strip (c) and stick on the fleshy part of the thumb. The tape is taken around the outside of the thumb, the fist clenched and then taped diagonally round the joint towards the little finger. Make a fist.

Eight strips (d) are now stuck in sequence across the back of the hand. Finish the operation with a strip (e) taken twice

110

around the wrist. It should be noted that the plaster tape must not be applied over the knuckles.

Warming Up

With bandages on, the boxer should warm up and go through his repertoire of stretching exercises and a few minutes on the pads, with the coach emphasising the simple tactics for that particular contest. After the warm-up, he should wrap up warmly in his gown, concentrating now on the tactics to follow and await the call to the ring. A towelling undergown is useful for retaining body heat as well as keeping sweat and grease off the ring robe.

At the Ringside

The amateur boxer and the professional boxing four and six rounds are restricted to two seconds in the corner, although in amateur boxing only one may talk to the boxer. For professional championships, up to four seconds are allowed to work the corner. The four will probably include the manager, the trainer or coach, a specialist cut repair man and an assistant second. However, whatever the code, the principles of corner work remain the same.

Before the boxer goes down to the ring it is advisable that the assistant second checks out the corner equipment (spitoon, water buckets) and position of ring steps etc. The following items of personal equipment are essential:

> White second's jacket
> White trousers or track suit bottoms and training
>   shoes
> Sterile gauze squares
> Swab sticks

Cotton wool
Cetavlex solution – 1 per cent
Adhesive wound dressings
Dumb-bell sutures
Adrenalin chloride 1-1000
Nobecutaine spray
Varidase or Ananase tablets
Crepe and cotton bandages
Scissors
Clean sponge and plastic water bottle
Ice bag and bucket
Nasal drops
For professional boxing only
   Medicated petroleum jelly

On arrival at the ring, most boxers require a drink to alleviate the dryness in the mouth which accompanies pre-fight tension. The assistant second should take care that the water bucket for the sponge is clean, and rinse the gumshield ready for the opening round. Thereafter his job will be to pass up the clean sponge and water bottle and rinse the gumshield. Prior to the opening bell the coach will keep the advice simple, and on the bell he will sit at the ring-side concentrating his attention on the opponent. Between rounds, the advice to the boxer should be kept to no more than two basic points and should not be given until he is seated in a relaxed position with his hands in his lap. Where more than two seconds are involved, the coach should stand in front of the boxer. In amateur boxing, precious time is saved if the coach leans through the ropes. Take care not to smother the boxer in the corner – give him time to let his breathing rate return to normal before giving his mouth a rinse. Before the bell, make sure he has been freshened up with a damp personal sponge or spray, and slip the freshly-washed gumshield into his mouth.

The fight can be won or lost in the corner, so make sure that the team is organised so that everybody has a function. If the boxer sustains a cut during the round the injury should have priority when he comes back to the corner. Sterile gauze should be used to clean up and examine the extent of the injury. If the cut is not serious, the adrenaline-soaked swab stick should be applied with pressure. This is the only coagulant permitted by both A.B.A. and B.B.B. of C. rules. In the professional ring *only*, medicated petroleum jelly may be applied to help contain the injury when the bleeding has been stopped by the adrenaline. This *may not be used* in amateur boxing. The ice bag should be on hand to apply to bruises and swellings both during and after the fight.

Throughout proceedings, do make sure that the sponge is kept clean and avoid the practice of a friendly wipe of the opponent's face – this is a sure way to spread infection. The sponge should be kept away from open wounds at all costs.

At the end of a contest, if you have taught him well, your boxer will accept the decision whichever way it goes. Be modest in victory and generous in defeat. Immediately after the fight it is best not to analyse either victory or loss. Perhaps the next session at the gym, when both boxer and coach are free of the euphoria or depression, is the best time to analyse the faults in technique and tactics and to work on the corrections. Any weak spots in defence and attack must be remedied before the next contest. Any lack of stamina, speed or strength must be corrected. If the will to win is weak, it must be cultivated. The coach must also carefully consider whether his own advice during the fight was correct.

Success in the Ring

Competition Equipment

Coming up to fight time, there is little doubt that the boxer's self-image is a most important factor in the mental approach to the forthcoming battle. It is, therefore, a great confidence boost, generating a feeling of wellbeing, to leave behind the bulky yet functional gymnasium clothing and change into sparkling clean ring attire.

Boxing Trunks

Make sure that these are a correct fit, around the waist particularly. A tight waistband interferes with your breathing and recovery in that vital minute's rest in the corner. Also make sure that the size of your trunks allows room for your foulproof protector.

Vests

If you are an amateur boxer, make sure you chose the snug-fitting variety that does not have shoulder straps likely to slip at a critical moment in the contest.

Socks

Avoid blisters by wearing white woollen socks. Too much nylon or other man-made fibres can cause the feet to sweat excessively. In a long fight, the constant rubbing will cause blistering on the ball of the foot.

114

Boxing Boots

The non-slip-soled boots are now the most effective, and care should be taken to wear them in at the gymnasium before using them in competition. Clean white laces help to improve the appearance.

Bandages

Amateurs should avoid the practice of using their training bandages in the competition ring and keep a new pair of crepe or cotton velpeau bandages for these special occasions. Training bandages should not be stuffed in the bag at the end of the session. Avoid sore hands by rolling and drying them after training.

Ring Robes

It is always advisable to wear a towelling gown underneath a smart velvet or satin robe to keep the body warm after the all-important warm-up, especially if you are boxing in a large cold hall.

Lonsdale Super Protector

A well-fitting protector is essential and should last your entire ring career. For the beginner there are cheaper versions.

Ready for the ring.
Note the hooded
towelling
undergown used to
keep in body heat
after warm-up. It
also protects the
satin gown from
sweat and grease

116

Gumshields

Perhaps the most important item in a boxer's equipment is a snug-fitting gumshield. For the novice the titan mouthguard is very effective, but the serious boxer should invest in the made-to-measure version.

Competition ring at the National Sporting Club

The Competitive Spirit and Mental Preparation

The coach should recognise that, although his boxer may have trained diligently and is strong in all the areas of physical condition, his true ability will be reflected in the way he produces his skills under the extreme stress of top competition. The good boxer digs deep into often

117

unsuspected resources to reveal his true worth in the ring. 'When the going gets tough, the tough get going.' This American expression best sums up the type of spirit required for ultimate success.

Tom McNab, the distinguished athletics coach and author, rightly suggests that 'Defeat lies not in failing to win gold medals or world championships, but in achieving less than you had a right to expect of yourself. The ultimate battle is always within, and you must find and explore the mechanisms which trigger off peak performances.'

Coaches are becoming increasingly aware that mere skill and physical condition are often not enough to achieve success in the Olympic and World Championship arena. The training of the mind to produce the peak performance now goes far beyond the level of pep talks by the coach. Such talks are often more use as an emotional relief for the nervous coach than as help to the boxer, who is himself usually undergoing a degree of mental torment prior to leaving the safety of the dressing room for the ring.

Such is the vast range of difference in the individual characteristics of boxers that no set approach can be laid down for the coach to encourage the right mental attitude that will leave the boxer best equipped to show his worth. For some a quiet word of encouragement is needed, for others a sharp word designed to stimulate, and for many the best solution is just to leave them alone.

Each boxer has a different level of mental arousal. Without doubt, to produce a performance of any quality a certain pitch of nervous tension is necessary; the adrenalin needs to be flowing, yet under control. Boxing is unique in that the

118

pre-contest tension is usually so intense that many boxers sustain such a loss of nervous energy that their performance is drained of sharpness and confidence. It was said that many of the fighters who faced the legendary Joe Louis were overcome by such a feeling of impending doom and sheer terror that they required considerable persuasion to leave the sanctuary of the toilet when the call to ring was due!

For all boxers, this battle with the inner self has to be overcome before the sound of that first bell. It is now fashionable to refer to this mental struggle as the inner game. The self-doubt about skill and physical condition that surfaces as the fight approaches must be banished by a positive approach. The inner game must be won.

Mental rehearsal drills, designed to enable the boxer to concentrate on the task in hand, should become a part of his immediate pre-fight routine. Following the dressing room warm-up and stretch ritual, the boxer should be left alone to build up a mental picture of the impending contest, imposing his own attacking strategies as positive counters to his opponent's offensive moves. This routine is important and requires great concentration, but it will help create the right environment or psychological 'set' for his performance. Unless the routine is established as a dressing room pre-bout ritual, many boxers will be overcome by a 'condemned cell' atmosphere that can prevail if care is not taken.

Although mental rehearsal and relaxation drills are important, there is no substitute for motivation. The desire to win has to be paramount and with it an eagerness to achieve certain standards of technical performance.

119

Recognising the degree of motivation in boxers is often difficult. I recall the performance of Chris Finnegan at the 1968 Mexico Olympics where at first the coach failed to identify the motivation and ambition that carried him through five hard bouts to win the Middleweight Gold Medal. He later admitted that it was a desire to become 'somebody' and not just a 'silly old brick-layer' that drove him on against the Russian Kiseliev in a desperately close Olympic final.

There was no questioning Chris Finnegan's physical fitness to compete at 7,500 feet in the rarified atmosphere of Mexico City against a field of international Middleweights. However there is little doubt that his success was a tribute to his mental approach which became more positive with each succeeding bout, enabling him to concentrate on making the most of his southpaw skills. Despite the intensity of the competition, Chris Finnegan won the inner game and with it Britain's last boxing Gold Medal.

The Boxer and His Weight

For many years the medical profession has warned boxers about the dangers of excessive weight reduction by crash dieting and by excessive 'drying out'. The young boxer often deludes himself that boxing at a weight below the one to which he is accustomed will give him a better chance of success. The good coach should have sufficient knowledge in this area to decide on the boxer's most effective weight in relation to his body composition. He will, of course, understand the effects of drastic weight reduction and if it is in the best interests of the boxer to lose some weight he will prescribe a sensible method.

Body Composition

To decide the optimum weight for a boxer, the best method is to examine his body composition in terms of the amount of muscle tissue (lean bodyweight) and the percentage of body fat in the total bodyweight. This is far more reliable than using standard height-weight charts.

Coaches should determine the percentage fat content of the body by measuring the amount of fat under the skin (subcutaneous fat) in selected areas of the body, i.e. at the back of the arm, just below the shoulder blades and just above the hip. Although skin callipers provide the most accurate measurements, the pinch grip (thumb and forefinger) on the back of the arm gives a good estimate of the amount of

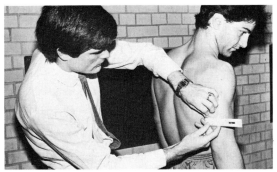

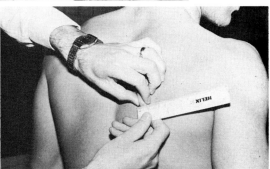

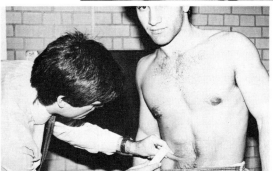

Measuring the amount of fat under the skin (subcutaneous fat) in selected areas – the back of the arm, just below the shoulder blade, and above the hip – by use of the pinch grip and ruler

122

subcutaneous fat. Experts have suggested that the total 'sub q' fat from the three measurement areas in a well-conditioned boxer should be 18-25 millimetres maximum.

Training increases the proportion of muscle tissue and decreases the proportion of 'sub q' fat in the total body weight. It therefore follows that for long-term weight reduction a balanced training programme and a suitable diet is the recommended method, and not drastic sweating which simply reduces the vital water content of the body for a temporary period only.

Research has distinguished between body stores and body reserves. Body stores are the fats or carbohydrates, in the body that can be used for energy without disturbing the machinery of the body. Carbohydrate stores are used for energy, and if these fall below a certain level, the body's normal activities will be impaired.

It has been estimated that the average young male has about 15 per cent body fat. In contrast, most well-conditioned male athletes have about 7 per cent body fat. An average young male weighing 81 kg has a total body fat content of about 12 kg (15 per cent of 81). He can therefore lose about 6.8 kg of fat (not lean tissue) without disturbing body functions. At his new weight of 74.2 kg he has 7 per cent body fat. But a well-conditioned athlete weighing 81 kg with a body fat content of 9 per cent (about 2 percentage points over the standard) can lose only 1.8 kg of fat (down to 7 per cent) without disturbing body functions.

These figures can be used as a guide for the boxer working sensibly at a long-term reduction of the fat content of the

123

body. However, he must beware the pitfalls of semi-starvation and dehydration. If he uses his energy reserves in training and does not replace the energy expenditure by food intake, his body will begin to use his protein reserves (muscle tissue) for energy. The loss of muscle tissue will reduce his strength. Semi-starvation results in a rapid decrease in the body's carbohydrate stores (a major energy store when exercising). This will result in a rapid loss in weight, but with a feeling of lethargy and lack of energy in the boxer.

Effects of Drastic Reduction

Too often the boxer will postpone a determined and sensible dieting programme to make the weight until he is left with no alternative but semi-starvation and greatly reduced water intake. One physiological effect of starvation diets is to upset the acid balance by seriously decreasing the blood alkaline, which acts as a buffer against fatigue and helps tolerate oxygen debt during competition.

The total carbohydrate content of the body varies between 400 and 500 grams (1,600 to 2,000 calories). These available stores of energy are exhausted in two to three hours of strenuous activity. During starvation, the stores are exhausted quickly, and the body therefore has to rely solely on its fat stores for energy. When fat is metabolised, ketone acid byproducts appear in the blood and urine and reduce blood alkaline. Fat cannot be metabolised as fast as carbohydrate, so energy production is slow; the result is early fatigue and general lack of endurance. Other biochemical effects of a starvation diet are a decrease in the blood glucose, which is associated with low energy levels, early fatigue, and a breakdown of muscle cells through

124

potassium loss. Because the drastic reduction in food intake usually accompanies hard training, boxers experience a dramatic decrease in endurance and a significant deterioration in speed and hand-eye co-ordination.

Adolescent boxers who continually neglect a balanced diet can expect to experience (a) a decrease in muscular endurance, (b) poor mental alertness, (c) early general fatigue, (d) an inability to put together punch combinations and (e) an inability to avoid punches and a corresponding inability to resist the effects of a punch.

The coach should therefore be well versed in the symptoms of early fatigue, irritability, and decreased ability to concentrate. No one wants to coach a boxer who looks good in the first round, begins to fade and look out-thought and outmanoeuvred in the second, and is hard pressed to survive the third.

The Effects of Drying Out

Perhaps the most widely practised method of reducing weight in boxing is the combination of reduced liquid intake with forced sweating in sweat suits and sauna baths. The use of laxatives is a final, desperate measure to bring a boxer down to the weight limit. The ease with which fluid can be reduced misleads some coaches and boxers. Although doctors, physiologists, and informed coaches have universally condemned such practices, they are not uncommon at major international competitions.

Body fluid is not necessarily excess weight, and it is very important to maintain the body's fluid balance. The movement of food and electrolytes and the transfer of gases in the tissues depend on fluid content to bathe cells. Because a loss of just a few pounds of body fluid can upset the efficiency of athletic performance, the fluid balance must not be tampered with.

A dehydrated boxer is likely to suffer a reduction in the volume of blood circulating. The heart rate must increase to try to maintain optimum cardiac output. Furthermore, the reduction in blood volume reduces heat transfer from the deeper body tissues to the skin, and the core body temperature rises. Unless quickly made up, the salt loss accompanying excessive sweating can also have marked and unpleasant effects, such as muscle cramps in the arms and legs, headaches, nausea, and diarrhoea.

If fluid levels decrease drastically, sweating may cease and body core temperatures may rise, resulting in heat exhaustion, hyperthermia and other disorders.

The reduction in blood volume greatly limits stamina and muscular endurance, the vital factors in a three-round contest. Medical authorities are also concerned about possible damage to kidney function; many older boxers, who are known to have used drastic measures to lose weight, have shown a tendency towards kidney disease in later life.

A Sensible Approach to Weight Reduction

The coach must accept that it is better to give away height and reach to an opponent than to delude one's charge that he can remain strong at a weight he must struggle to make.

It is far better to think in terms of building strength, speed, and stamina at a weight at which he can box with maximum efficiency. For those boxers who obviously carry excess subcutaneous fat, there are two ways to lose weight safely: one is to reduce the total calorie intake through a well-balanced diet, and the other is to exercise sensibly. Combining the two has maximum effect.

During the weight reduction period it is important for the boxer to be capable of maintaining a high level of physical training.

When body weight is lost rapidly over a short period of time the loss of body fat is minimal. However, losses of carbohydrate energy stores, lean tissue and water can be substantial. Thus, a long-term structured weight control programme should be followed to maximise the loss of body fat whilst sparing the body's protein and carbohydrate stores. Weight loss should be limited to 0.5–1.0 kg per week, which would require an energy restriction in the range of 500–1,100 kcal daily (each kg of body fat is equal to approximately 7,700 kcal). However, body fat loss is best achieved through a combination of dietary restriction and aerobic exercise, which helps to burn existing fat for fuel. For example, a 91 kg boxer who carries 11.3 kg of excess fat but wants to box at 81 kg, could easily lose the 10 kg in 12 to 13 weeks. A reduction of 600 kcal in his daily food intake would result in a weekly deficit of 4,200 kcal and a loss of just over 0.5 kg of body fat a week. If he added six one-hour workouts that each burned 500 kcal, he would lose an additional 0.4 kg (3,000 kcal) of body fat per week, for a total loss of just over 0.9 kg per week.

The composition of a weight reduction diet should not differ from the recommendations for a normal athletic diet. An adequate intake of carbohydrate and protein is essential to maintain the body's energy stores and prevent an imbalance between protein synthesis and degradation. The contribution of carbohydrate to the diet should be in the range of 65–70% of total daily calorie intake.

Some coaches have found carbohydrate supplements, such as MAXIM, useful in the preparation of boxers for a major competition. As the training load increases, MAXIM, a powdered glucose polymer, provides an easily digestible source of carbohydrate energy which can be consumed during and between training sessions, helping to maintain the blood sugar level and delay the onset of fatigue. As the contest approaches and during a major competition when careful control of the diet is necessary, the measured portions of MAXIM allow an exact calculation of caloric value as part of a weight control strategy. Furthermore, consumption of MAXIM in the period after making the weight will replenish any carbohydrate stores that may have become depleted during weight making strategies.

Planning the Training Programme

In the past twenty years, great strides have been made in establishing physical and mental preparation for sporting competition on a more scientific basis. Boxing has long been accepted as a sport that requires rigorous training to bring its competitors to peak conditions for a contest. From its earliest beginnings and through the prize-fight era of the eighteenth and nineteenth centuries to the present day, there has been little change in training methods. Many of the training activities have been grossly unscientific and have no basis in current research into physical conditioning. Thus it is questionable whether the long-accepted routines pursued by such heroes as Dempsey, Louis and Ali have much place in the training programme of an amateur boxer who is being geared to box three rounds at a high work rate.

The problems of schedule planning for the amateur coach are many and complex, particularly as the amateur boxing season has long since spread from nine months to practically the whole year round. The coach must therefore work on a long-term development plan for a four-year period, also a yearly plan, and then the more immediate preparation plans for the build-up to an imminent competition. The content of the programme should be geared to the individual needs of boxers in his club so that they may realise their full potential. He must therefore consider the following:

1. The age and physical maturation of the boxer – junior boxers should not work on a 'young adults' training routine.

2. The ambition and dedication of the boxer; motivation and rate of learning; the restrictions imposed by his job or education or his availability for training.

3. His own availability as a coach – how many sessions per week can he devote himself to the boxers?

4. Which energy systems should receive the most training stress in the schedules – this will differ widely within the club and depends on the physiological make-up of each boxer.

5. The availability of club premises and how much space and equipment is available.

6. Not least, the climate – in certain areas, the morning run will be dependent on the temperature and weather conditions.

A cursory glance at these factors is enough to emphasise that it would be impossible to lay down a schedule for everyone to follow and expect good results from all boxers in the club. The coach must therefore look at each individual in terms of their development over a four-year period as well as their development in the forthcoming year. Each boxer should have his attainment objectives set before him, whether they be seen in terms of Olympic gold medals or winning Divisional Championships. With these objectives in mind, the coach can settle down to plan a sensible development programme. This looking ahead is particularly important for the young teenager, who should be set attainable objectives over this development period. It should also be remembered that enjoyment should be the keynote in the coaching of the young boxer of school age. Competition in these early stages of learning should be restricted, and incentives carefully planned. Coaches who have failed to heed advice and planned rigorous routines for their youngsters with schoolboy championships as an end in themselves, have been doomed to disappointment when their charges have left the sport, worn out mentally and physically, without realising their potential.

The Yearly Programme

Having looked at the long-term objectives, the coach should now draw up his yearly programme, bearing in mind that it would be unreasonable to expect his boxer to reach a high peak of emotional and physical fitness more than three times in the year. These peaks should obviously be planned to coincide with the most important objectives for that particular season. Thus, if a major international competition dominates the year the coach should plan this as the main objective and build up to it accordingly.

Peak fitness can only be held for a short time. Any schedule attempting to sustain the length of time by keeping the boxers at maximum training performances will inevitably produce 'staleness', therefore much of the season will require boxers to reach a series of smaller peaks. Thus after some relatively intense interval work in the period leading up to a bout, the coach would decrease the intensity after the bout and probably prescribe a complete break and change of environment for a few days before leading up to another bout. There obviously can be no hard and fast rule and the coach's approach may be modified to suit the

131

individual personality and the number of boxers that come under his care.

With this background in mind, the coach should now decide which physical factor should have priority in the programme without neglecting the technical skills. He should by now have evaluated the task and decided where and in what months he should be laying emphasis on the following:

1. Aerobic training.

2. Anaerobic training.

3. Muscular endurance.

4. Power.

5. General strength.

6. Speed.

7. Flexibility.

8. Technical skill.

Close Season – 2-3 Months

This is the period at the end of the major competitions, but it will vary according to the event that is going to be the peak for that particular season. Allowing for a short break for boxers and coach, this is the time of year where 'the medals are won'. For the boxer who has finished a busy season, this is the time to get away from the gym and to seek a complete change of training environment. Training should now take him outdoors where the emphasis should be on steady state or aerobic running, with enjoyment being a key factor. At this time the boxer should run over the country with the occasional Fartlek (Speed Play) run thrown in for good measure. This should take place three days per week, with weight training and circuit training taking up the other three days. With the weights the emphasis should be on muscle endurance. For variety this is also the time for a suitably designed individual circuit. Throughout this period the boxer should on no account neglect his warm-up and flexibility routines.

Pre-season – 2 Months

The running sessions should now be over a set distance designed to build up a reservoir of cardio-vascular fitness. Here the boxer should concentrate on an even pace but try to improve his time over distance from one to three miles. The weight training – three times per week – should now be concentrated on general strength with the repetitions cut down and the set system introduced. To add variety to the programme, fixed-load circuits should also be used; and gymnasium work should commence with the emphasis on endurance, using 3 to $3\frac{1}{2}$ minute rounds for bag work, skiping and shadow boxing. Again flexibility work precedes and closes every session.

Early and Mid-season – 2 Months

The emphasis should now be applied to speed and endurance training, thus a gradual transition to interval work should take place. The running should be devoted to the interval method, using the track if one is available. Here the recovery times should be watched carefully and the distances gradually cut to below 400 metres, at the start of the period, to 150 metres – with speed becoming imperative. For a change of 'diet' and to avoid the monotony of track work, uphill runs and the occasional

133

'Fartlek' should be prescribed.

Weight training sessions should be reduced to twice a week, using fewer repetitions but heavier weights. Gym sessions should also be phased into the interval system, reducing the length of rounds and decreasing the rest intervals. Sparring, of course, should never be reduced to less than two-minute rounds because of the danger in abandoning technical skills in favour of mindless aggression. To supplement the strength and stamina work, Target Training Circuits can be introduced as the peak season phase approaches. Again, flexibility routines are an integral part of all sessions.

Peak Season — The Remainder of the Competitive Season

The peak competitive season should see the culmination of the coach's schedule. At this stage the body, by process of adaptation, is now capable of a fierce diet of interval work with the emphasis strictly on speed. Only if the work load of the previous phases has been undertaken, will the boxer respond to the stress work of the early part of peak season work. The running sessions should consist of interval sprinting in the shape of three sets 15×15 seconds runs and pyramid sprints reducing the distances to 60 metres.

The power work enters a maintenance period of two sessions per week with two different schedules to add variety. Further variety can be added with circuit training in the form of Target and Ton-up circuits.

In the gym, high-quality interval work predominates, with technique always very important when working on bag, pads or sparring. As a particular contest nears, the last ten days remain a maintenance or sharpening period. At this

134

stage the work has been done and no purpose is served in 'boiling the kettle dry', thus taking the boxer over the prescribed peak.

Before all sessions flexibility work, particularly at the hip and shoulder joint, should be carried out. The warming down process at the end of all heavy training sessions should also be observed diligently.

Having reached the end of the year's schedule, the coach should now review the work and should not be afraid to be self-critical in the eternal search for improvement. He should encourage the boxers to keep training diaries and to evaluate the work that they have been doing.

Conclusion

In this brief excursion into a very complex field, some of the principles and methods that should guide a coach in planning a training programme have been set out. No attempt has been made to lay out a specific schedule because any such schedule is useless except in relation to the needs of the particular boxer for whom it is designed. There are many who have reservations about a coach setting schedules in advance for a boxer unless he can supervise every day. If he cannot supervise every session, the coach should explain to the boxer the principles behind the programme so that the boxer can eventually devise his own schedule. From this point the coach's role is to supply advice and encouragement. Research into the physiology of human athletic performance continues and there are many areas of training method that are still matters of opinion. It is imperative, therefore, that a coach should always examine critically the effect of his training of the boxer and experiment judiciously with new ideas.

Gallery of Champions

The following pages offer a small selection of fighters from the past quarter of a century. These men have helped provide the sensations and drama that make boxing such a special sport.

Although the term has been misused, it would be right and proper to describe some of these boxers as Great Champions.

Muhammad Ali

Previously known as Cassius Clay. Three times holder of the World Heavyweight Championship, boxed in London three times — twice against Henry Cooper and once against Brian London. He was considered by many to be the greatest heavyweight of all time.

Cassius Clay first attracted world attention when he won the Olympic Gold Medal at Light Heavyweight in 1960. The ease with which he beat former Olympic Middleweight champion Schatkov (Russia) and finalist Pietrzykowski (Poland), two seasoned iron curtain 'professionals', clearly indicated that an exceptional talent had arrived.

Clay changed his name to Muhammad Ali shortly after his huge upset win over the fearsome Sonny Liston. After swiftly demolishing Liston in the return match, Ali proceeded to dazzle and defeat all the available contenders of the sixties. He was stripped of his title in 1967 for refusing to be conscripted into the US Army. Making his return to the ring in 1970 and despite a loss to Joe Frazier, Ali clearly beat all the contenders of the day, including Frazier, to land a title chance against the immensely powerful George Foreman whom he defeated in an epic fight in Zaire. Unfortunately Ali was no longer the dancing, consummate boxing artist, and in defeating all the hard punching challengers, including the likes of Frazier, Lyle, Shavers and Norton in the seventies, he absorbed too much punishment. Despite losing and regaining the title to Leon Spinks he was a sad shadow of a great boxer when he suffered a one-sided defeat against Larry Holmes in 1980.

Not since the days of Joe Louis had one man commanded such worldwide attention in the often seamy world of prize fighting.

Riddick Bowe

Former IBF and WBA Heavyweight Champion, born in the same tough Brownsville area of New York as Mike Tyson, Bowe won a World Junior title as an amateur. He later won a Silver Medal at Super Heavyweight in the 1988 Olympic Games, being stopped in the final by Lennox Lewis. A talented large heavyweight, Bowe defeated all the leading heavyweight contenders and in November 1992 defeated Evander Holyfield in a fiercely contested fight for the WBC, WBA and IBF titles. After two farcical mismatches, Bowe forced the return challenge of the highly motivated underdog Evander Holyfield who fought an inspirational battle to kill off any hope Bowe may have entertained of facing Lennox Lewis for a highly lucrative unification fight.

138

Dave Charnley

The Dartford southpaw, seen here bravely giving weight away to World Welterweight Champion, **Emile Griffith**. Charnley, European, Commonwealth and British Lightweight Champion 1957-65, was perhaps one of the best in the history of British boxing never to win a world title. He twice challenged American Joe Brown, the second a bitterly fought fifteen rounds that many thought he had won.

By way of consolation Charnley knocked out Brown in six rounds in a third meeting, after the American had lost his title. In an era of outstanding lightweight boxers Charnley fought and beat most of the leading contenders including Kenny Lane, Len Matthews and Paul Armistead. In the early sixties Charnley repelled all British contenders including Dave 'Darkey' Hughes in a record 40 seconds, Joe Lucy and later Maurice Cullen. Charnley retired from the ring in 1965 unbeaten British Lightweight Champion.

139

John Conteh

British, Commonwealth, European and World Light-Heavyweight Champion 1973-78. The first British boxer since Freddie Mills to win the world championship at this weight, Conteh retained his crown on three occasions. Before affairs outside the ring overtook him, he rated as one of the best box fighters produced in this country since the war.

140

Henry Cooper

European, British and Commonwealth Champion 1959-70, weighing in for the defence of his European Championship against **Jose Urtain** of Spain. Easily Britain's best post-war heavyweight, Henry made a determined assault on Ali's world crown in 1966, having startled Ali and the boxing world three years earlier by flooring him with his celebrated left hook. However, his old bugbear, a tendency to cut easily, ended his challenge in the sixth round.

141

Cooper had dominated the British heavyweight scene after an uncertain start in the mid-fifties when he lost to Joe Bygraves, Joe Erskine and Ingemar Johansson. During the next ten years Cooper defeated all the British contenders of the day, recording impressive wins over Joe Erskine, Brian London, Billy Walker, Jack Bodell and Johnny Prescott. An emphatic win over Piero Tomasoni in 1969 in defence of his European title clearly established him as the best heavyweight on this side of the Atlantic in the year that he was awarded the O.B.E. A very controversial points loss to a young Joe Bugner in 1971 caused a disappointed Henry Cooper to retire.

Adrian Dodson

Formerly an amateur of some distinction who learnt much of his boxing in the United States, Dodson, born in Guyana, represented his native country in the 1988 Olympics eventually losing in the quarter finals. Also qualifying as English, Dodson was selected to represent Great Britain in the Barcelona Olympics of 1992. Struggling to make the welterweight limit Dodson registered one win only to lose in the next round. Now unbeaten as a pro, Dodson looks to make his name as an outstanding light middleweight.

Terry Downes

World and British Middleweight Champion 1958-62, seen here shaking hands with a young **Bernard Hart**, now Managing Director of Lonsdale Sports, himself a former welterweight of some promise. The dashing, crashing, smashing Downes won and lost his title in hard battles with American Paul Pender. His whirlwind style of non-stop punching made him a tremendous draw. Three years after losing to Pender, Terry made a tremendous effort to gain a second world title by challenging Willie Pastrono, only to be stopped in round eleven when ahead on points.

144

Chris Eubank

WBO Super Middleweight Champion. Former undefeated WBO and WBC International Middleweight Champion. Never a national champion, Eubank currently holds the record for having more successful world title wins than any British fighter in history. He won his first title, the WBC International Middleweight title against Hugo Corti in 1990, but sprang to international prominence in a wildly exciting 'grudge' fight against Nigel Benn when, calling on all his reserves, he stopped his opponent in the ninth round. After retaining his title against Michael Watson with a debatable points decision, Eubank faced Watson again for the vacant WBO Super Middleweight and came back from near defeat to stop Watson in the final round of a fight that nearly ended tragically. Taking time to decide whether he wished to continue, Eubank remains undefeated to date having faced a series of undistinguished challengers but still managing to outpoint Nigel Benn in a much disputed return.

145

Chris Finnegan

European, British and Commonwealth Light Heavyweight Champion. Olympic Middleweight Gold Medallist, Mexico City 1968. A clever southpaw, Finnegan astounded critics by winning the Olympic Middleweight title in 1968 – no British boxer has come near to winning a gold medal since. As a professional, he employed a more aggressive style and although he lacked power of punch he briefly dominated the Light-Heavyweight division in Europe and qualified for a world title fight against the talented American Bob Foster. Without the punch to trouble Foster, Finnegan waged a courageous battle until the referee stopped the fight in the fourteenth round.

146

Bob Foster

World Light-Heavyweight Champion 1968-74, seen working on the speed ball in training for his title defence against Chris Finnegan in 1972. A supreme boxer, he knocked out Dick Tiger in four rounds to win the title, and made no fewer than fourteen successful defences of his championship. His only defeats were suffered at the hands of heavyweights of the calibre of Ali and Frazier.

147

Herol Graham

Former undefeated British, Commonwealth and European Light-Middleweight Champion. Graham won the British championship from Pat Thomas in 1981, and relinquished his three championships in 1984 in order to concentrate on the middleweight division and challenge Marvin Hagler for the world crown. A throwback to the old school of clever boxers that abounded in the 1930s, Graham narrowly failed in a world title challenge for the middleweight title held by

Mike McCallum when the effective body punching of the Jamaican-born champion took its toll in the final rounds. In his last world title challenge against the hard punching Julian Jackson, Graham gave a dazzling exhibition of precision punching in the early rounds only to make the classic mistake of trying to stop his now cut and desperate opponent. Graham, with the title his for the taking, walked into a wild counter that felled him for the count leaving him concussed for several minutes. Although Graham continued his career with wins against modest opposition the loss of his middleweight title to Frank Grant, the first British boxer to beat him in fourteen years, persuaded him to retire from the ring.

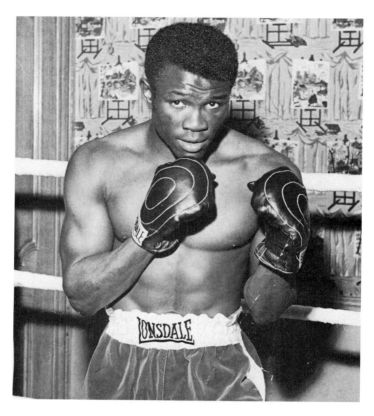

Emile Griffith

World Welter- and Middleweight Champion 1961-65, a brilliant box fighter who came to Britain to defend his welter title against Welshman, Brian Curvis. Griffith had a long career and for over a decade clashed with the big names in the middle and welter divisions. His record serves as a 'who's who' of the era with Benny 'Kid' Paret, Luis Rodriguez, Nino Benvenuti, Dick Tiger, Carlos Monzon and Alan Minter all sharing the ring with him.

Maurice Hope

World, European, British and Commonwealth Light-Middleweight Champion 1974-81. A strong southpaw, 1972 Olympic quarter finalist, Hope won the world title from Rocky Mattioli in San Remo in eight rounds. He successfully defended the championship five times, eventually losing to Wilfredo Benitez (USA).

151

Lennox Lewis

British born but resident in Canada when he launched his amateur career, Lewis has reserved his place in history as the first British World Heavyweight Champion this century. An outstanding amateur, Lewis won a Gold Medal at the inaugural World Junior Championships. He represented Canada in two Olympic Games winning the Super Heavyweight Gold Medal at Seoul in 1988, stopping Riddick Bowe in the final.

As a professional, Lennox Lewis was impressive in stopping the dangerous Razor Ruddock in a final eliminator which quickly led to Riddick Bowe renouncing his newly won WBC belt rather than defend it against Lennox. Lewis, fresh from wins over Tony Tucker and Frank Bruno, now looks to a lucrative unification fight against Evander Holyfield.

Charlie Magri

World Flyweight Champion 1983, European and British
Flyweight Champion 1977-81, seen here winning one of his
three A.B.A. titles. A game, aggressive, two-fisted battler,
Charlie has been one of our most popular flyweight
champions.

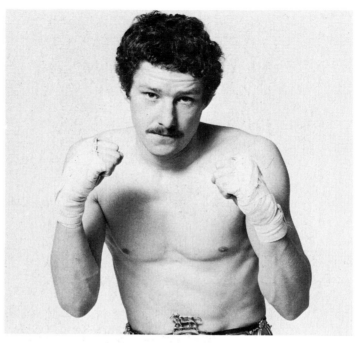

Terry Marsh

I.B.F. World Light Welterweight Champion 1987. British and European Light Welterweight Champion. Marsh, a former Royal Marine, was an outstanding amateur as a schoolboy and junior and twice holder of the ABA Welterweight Championship. Bitterly disappointed at not being selected for the Moscow Olympic Games, Marsh turned professional. His upright skilful boxing style, based on an excellent defence and a fine left jab, took him to the British and European titles. Marsh's display in stopping the American Joe Louis Manley to win the world title amazed critics who had doubted his ability to punch with such venom and variety.

Barry McGuigan

The WBA World Featherweight Champion 1985–86 Barry McGuigan must rate alongside Turpin and Conteh as one of the finest box-fighters produced in the British Isles. A brilliant amateur from Clones in Northern Ireland, McGuigan won a Commonwealth Games Gold Medal in Edmonton in 1978 at Bantamweight and represented Ireland in the Moscow Olympics in 1980. As a professional

155

fighter McGuigan was a wicked body puncher and, although troubled with knuckle injury problems throughout his career, became a magnetic draw at the major Belfast venues, the Ulster and Kings Halls. His path to the Championship was littered with knockouts and stoppages. Fight followers from Northern Ireland, both Catholic and Protestant, were united behind their man and flocked to London to see him beat Eusebio Pedroza for the title. Two successful defences followed against Taylor and Cabrera, but an ill-fated defence against Steve Cruz (USA) in the Nevada desert proved disastrous. Fighting in the midday sun to meet television schedules, McGuigan bravely defied the intense heat to lose his title on a close decision. A brief comeback following a bitter managerial dispute saw McGuigan announce his retirement in 1989.

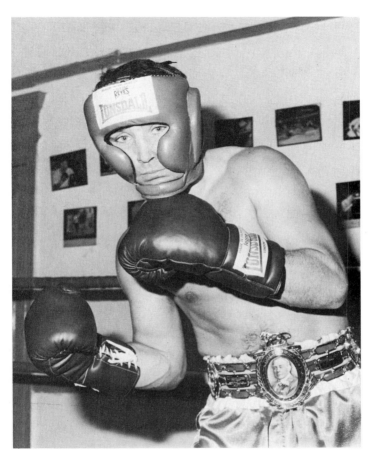

Alan Minter

World, European and British Middleweight Champion,
1975-81. A solid punching southpaw, Minter, Olympic
bronze medallist in 1972, won the world title in Las Vegas
where he outpointed Vito Antuofermo. He lost the title to
Marvin Hagler in London when he was stopped on cuts
after three rounds.

157

Ken Norton

Proclaimed W.B.C. Heavyweight Champion in 1978, but lost to Larry Holmes three months later. A fine, well-built boxer, Norton was one of the few fighters to beat Muhammad Ali, breaking his jaw in the process. He later challenged George Foreman for the title, but was stopped in two rounds in Caracas.

Carlos Ortiz

World Light-Welter and Lightweight Champion 1959-68.
An excellent stand-up fighter, Ortiz was one of the finest
American boxers to appear in this country and made a
lasting impression when he clearly outpointed Dave
Charnley on the last show held at the famous Harringey
Arena in 1958. He returned in 1963 to outpoint Maurice
Cullen at Wembley, but was stopped by another British
fighter, Ken Buchanan, in his last fight in 1972 in New
York.

159

Willie Pep

World Featherweight Champion 1942-50. Willie, seen here coaching some young hopefuls in London, was one of the most accomplished champions of all time. Nicknamed 'Willie the Wisp', most of his 229 professional wins took him the distance. His comeback points win over Sandy Saddler, following the loss of his title by a knockout, was regarded by many as one of the finest exhibitions of all-round boxing skill ever witnessed.

Pep started his long professional career at the age of 17 and won the New York State version of the featherweight title

160

when he was 20, holding the title for six years before encountering Saddler. Three more successful defences followed including a points win over Ray Famechon before he was forced to retire in the rubber match against Sandy Saddler in 1953. A series of comebacks were made but a loss to Hogan 'Kid' Bassey in 1958 clearly marked his end as a top class featherweight. Despite this a 43-year-old Pep made his final comeback in 1965 and recorded 9 wins in 10 bouts before being persuaded that he should take up refereeing.

Robin Reid

An outstanding amateur boxer from Warrington, Robin Reid more than justified his Olympic selection when he reached the semi-finals in Barcelona to crown his career with an Olympic Bronze Medal. Unbeaten as a professional, Reid looks to be an outstanding prospect for the future.

Sugar Ray Robinson

World Welter and Middleweight Champion 1946-60. Pound for pound, Robinson was probably boxing's best puncher of all time. He boxed for 25 years and fought 22 world championship contests. Relinquishing the Welterweight Championship which he gained from Tommy Bell in 1946, Robinson, who had outgrown the division, took the Middleweight Championship from Jake La Motta, stopping the Bronx Bull in impressive style. He narrowly missed becoming a triple titleholder when extreme heat forced his retirement against Joe Maxim in a Light-Heavyweight Championship fight in 1952. Robinson lost and regained his middleweight crown in fights with Randolph Turpin, Gene Fullmer, and Carmen Basilio. All three were epic battles, but still Robinson battled on until he finally retired at the age of 45 after some 201 fights.

163

A measure of Robinson's consummate skill and punishing power can be seen in the video of his return bout with the rugged Gene Fullmer when his perfect left hook counter knocked out the powerful champion in the 5th round of their Chicago title fight.

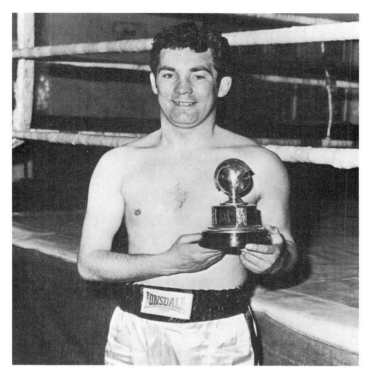

Howard Winstone

World, European and British Featherweight Champion 1961-68. The 'Welsh Wizard' from Merthyr was a master boxer, particularly with the left hand, in the best traditions of Jim Driscoll, an earlier Welsh folk hero who dominated the featherweight ranks. Winstone challenged three times for the world crown against the powerful Mexican, Vicente Saldivar. The second challenge at Cardiff following his brilliant battle at Earl's Court was exceedingly close, but it was a win against Mitsunori Seki for the title left vacant by Saldivar's retirement that finally brought the title to Wales.

165

Finding a Club

National Governing Bodies

English ABA
C. Brown (Secretary), Crystal Palace National Sports Centre, London SE19 2BB

Welsh ABA
J. Kerswell-Watkins (Hon. sec.), 8 Erw Wen, Rhwibina, Cardiff

Scottish ABA
F. Hendry (Hon. Sec.), 96 High Street, Lochee, Dundee

Irish ABA
A. O'Brien (Hon. Sec.), National Boxing Stadium, South Circular Road, Dublin 8

Canadian ABA
1600 James Naismith Drive, Gloucester, Ontario K1B 5N4

The Amateur Boxing Association of England Ltd Hon. Secretaries of Regional Associations

Season 1993/94

Eastern Counties ABA
D. Rulten, 8 Coventry Close, Colchester, Essex CO1 2RN
Tel: 0206 867299

Home Counties ABA
H. Brandwood, 88 Mount View, Henley on Thames, Oxon
RG9 2EL
Tel: 0491 578317

London ABA
C. Putt, 58 Comber Grove, Camberwell, London SE5 0LD
Tel: 071 252 7008

Midland Counties ABA
P. Blenkinsopp, 9 Hullbrook Road, Billesley, Birmingham
B13 0JU
Tel: 021 443 5103

North East Counties ABA
E. Hoyland, 23 Valley Road, Swinton, Nr Mexborough,
South Yorkshire S64 8JL
Tel: 0709 874436

North West Counties ABA
P. Hayes, 3 Limebrook Close, Openshaw, Manchester M11 1LH
Tel: 061 301 4085

Southern Counties ABA
J. Faulkner, 192 New Road, Copnor, Portsmouth, Hants PO2 7RW
Tel: 0705 829688

Western Counties ABA
A. R. Lyons, 4 Compton Close, Shepton Mallet, Somerset BA4 5QZ
Tel: 0749 342377

Combined Services BA
Maj. D. Sears, Secretary/Treasurer, c/o A.S.C.B., M Block, Clayton Barracks, Aldershot, Hants GU11 2BG
Tel: 0252 348581

Royal Navy BA
Lt. G. Bushell, Staff Recreational Officer, To Flight Officer to Scotland & N. Ireland, Maritime HQ, Pitreavie, Dunfermline, Fife KYL 5QE
Tel: 0383 412161 x 4396

Army BA
Maj. D. Sears – as Combined Services BA

Royal Air Force BA
Sqd. Ldr. B. Dean, RAF BA Secretary, HQ Strike Command, Supply 5A, RAF High Wycombe, Bucks HP14 4UE
Tel: 0494 461461 x 7414